PARTICIPATORY RURAL APPRAISAL

STUDIES IN RURAL PARTICIPATION

No.1: Participatory Rural Appraisal
Methodology and Applications
Neela Mukherjee

No.2: Readings in Rural Participation

No.3: Rural Habitat and Poverty — Whose Perceptions?

ABOUT THE AUTHOR

Dr. (Mrs.) Neela Mukherjee is currently working as a Professor of Economics at the Lal Bahadur Shastri National Academy of Administration, Mussoorie (Uttar Pradesh). In her pursuit of participatory development, Dr. Mukherjee has undertaken action-research, organised training courses in rural participatory methods and has directly conducted a large number of participatory sessions with villagers, in India and other developing countries. Some of her experiences have been described in this book.

Her other professional interests relate to the political economy of greenhouse gases and multilateral negotiations for trade in services. The main thrust of analysis underlying her areas of interest is democratization of development process and empowerment of poor, implications of which are both in terms of empowerment of poor and deprived individuals and that of the poor countries of the South. Dr. Mukherjee has written extensively in her areas of interest and she has a number of papers and a few books to her credit.

Studies in Rural Participation-1

PARTICIPATORY RURAL APPRAISAL

Methodology and Applications

NEELA MUKHERJEE

Professor of Economics

L.B.S. National Academy of Administration

Mussoorie (Uttar Pradesh)

India

CONCEPT PUBLISHING COMPANY, NEW DELHI-110059

ISBN 81-7022-473-X (HB)
ISBN 81-7022-637-6 (PB)

First Published 1993
Reprinted 1997, 1998, 2003

Published and Printed by
Ashok Kumar Mittal
Concept Publishing Company
A/15-16, Commercial Block, Mohan Garden
NEW DELHI-110059 (India)

Phones : 25351460, 25351794
Fax : 091-11-25357103
Email : publishing@conceptpub.com

To

B.N. Yugandhar

to

re-inforce

his bias

towards

People's Participation

in

Rural Development

PREFACE

The present book is neither a handbook nor a cookbook of rural participation. It is a mid-way documentation of an on-going process of direct participation based on the methodology of Participatory Rural Appraisal (PRA). It presents the principles, the methods applied and selected field experiences in applications of PRA. The book, is at best, an intermediate product of experiments in learning from the villagers and, at worst, a study in participation much of whose results are not in the nature of a 'blueprint' for replication and many of whose limits are unknown as yet.

I am not so sure whether there can be a final document on participation. Participation, by its nature varies in degrees, modes and kinds. The process of participation tends to be unique on every occasion and the kind and degree of participation also tend to differ. Different participative methods evolve in response to different situations and the product of participation changes from time to time and from location to location.

In any case, learning about rural participation from a book is surely an inferior way of gaining knowledge than learning about it from actual field situations. However, an inferior way is adopted in this case in absence of a better substitute. This is because, in a changing scenario, it is important to document the lessons learnt from the past for sharing of experiences with others. The book is primarily to share some of the PRA experiences from real life.

It is important to observe that participation of rural people is much easily said than done. It is not an easy process of involving them towards participatory development. At the same time, it is important to ask, what kind of a 'development' is that which does not interests its participants or involve them? Whom is this 'development' for where the clienteles merely act as passive spectators? Each participatory session with villagers makes us realise of how little we know of their perceptions and capabilities and yet with what zeal we endlessly pursue our self-designed rural development programmes year after year and decade after decade.

'Development' can be richer and meaningful only through the

participation of the clienteles of development. Here is the challenge of development which lies in the challenge of participation. It is a challenge for all those who act as 'facilitators' of development right from a policy maker down to a village level worker.

For the 'facilitators' of development such as the policy makers, the donors, the planners, the extension agents, the scientists and others there lies ahead a great scope for improvement in terms of understanding of development perspectives. The policy makers may wish to augment their world view of development and to experience the 'thrill' of participation in actual rural situations. This can be done by spending more time in field visits and through the practice of listening to villagers. Similarly, it would help the donors of developmental aid to listen directly to the rural people and to enlarge their 'world view' on rural issues.

For the development planners and administrators, it is important to solicit the participation of different groups of rural people not only on paper but also in reality. This will help the planners to ensure that their plans are realistic and participatory and their targets are people-oriented not object-oriented, where qualitative aspects of life are as much important as quantitative aspects. The development administrator's participation will primarily rest on his leadership to enthuse the field-level workers and involve the weak and the deprived in decision-making. The extension agents can gain from offering themselves the opportunity to learn from the clienteles of their extension work.

The non-governmental development organisations as partners in grass-root development can continuously search for better opportunities in participatory planning so as to redefine their objectives and modes of operation in collaboration with rural people.

The academicians, in the area of rural development, can seize the chance of being less 'bookish'. They can start by spending more time in villages to have a feel of rural people's 'world view' in order to realise why their theoretical models are unable to explain the intricacies of the real world situations and why their recommendations fail to answer the real issues involved.

Those agricultural scientists and the researchers confined to the laboratories and experimental farms cannot afford to remain behind. In their search for improving their research output they can also minimise their communication gap with their clienteles through participatory research with poor farmers.

At the end, I wish to mention that the readers may or may not enjoy reading this book and many questions arising in their minds would remain unanswered. There isn't a bagfull of answers to all the questions raised in the context of a participatory learning process. Some of the answers do exist while others would come from varied and better field experiences in future. The least I can suggest is not to miss any opportunity to communicate with rural people and learn from them.

My minimum expectation from writing this book would be fulfilled if many of our 'facilitators' of rural development, engaged in policy, action and research can realise that participation of rural people is possible and beneficial. They can then spread the message of participation from their own experiences.

Mussoorie

NEELA MUKHERJEE
2nd April, 1993

ACKNOWLEDGEMENTS

The study would not have been possible without the active support and cooperation of many individuals, groups and institutions. Each of them deserve mention not withstanding the length of the list which follows.

I am deeply indebted to the villagers of different villages who participated with great zeal and enthusiasm in the participatory sessions and contributed towards this book by way of knowledge, experience and analysis.

Villagers

Villagers of village Madhapur, District Ranga Reddy (Andhra Pradesh), India; Villagers of villages Panchkhuri, Munshipatna, Pathpur, Ketara, Moulara, Habla, Krishna Rakshit Chak, Kalsigeriya and Berapal, District Midnapore (West Bengal), India; Villagers of Villages Khanpur, Khoragorh and Baksha, District Hoogly (West Bengal), India; Villagers of villages Patkita, Barasini, Golcunda, Asurgariya, Astagora, Dhadka, Latapara and Velaidih, District Purulia (West Bengal), India; Villagers of villages Bhagwanpur, Bhaniyawala, Signiwala and Guddi, District Dehradun (Uttar Pradesh), India; Villagers of Ulloor village, District Trivandrum (Kerala), India; Villagers of village Dhobah, District Muzaffarpur (Bihar), India; Villagers of villages Jihu, Larhi, Ramgarh, Sijua and Barki, District Hazaribagh (Bihar) India; Villagers of villages Singhpur, Muri, Nawadih, Hasadih, Kulsadh, Lota and Banta Hajam, District Ranchi Bihar, India; Villagers of villages Zhadgarh and Awale, District Thane (Maharashtra), India.

Villagers of village Nlaphwane and village Zwenshambe, Botswana; Villagers of village Khalijani, Bansinagar and Banstaoli, district Tangail, Bangladesh; Villagers of Dakhinsalna, Ghazipur, Bangladesh.

There are many officials, friends and well-wishers who helped in various ways towards the present study and they deserve my sincere thanks. Their names are as follows:

B.N. Yugandhar, Dr. C.S. Prasad, Dr. Vijay Gupta, Sudhir K. Ghosh, Dr. Brijpal Singh, Professor D. Bannerjee, Dr. Gopal Iyer, Dr. Debu Bandyopadhyay, Lalit Mathur, V.K. Agnihotri, Avadash Kaushal, Anita Das, Badal Das, Jalaja Sinha, Sudhir Krishna, S. Mendiratta, R.C.S. Bisht, Manjula, Prem Kumari, Poonam, Santulan Choubey, Ramesh Subramanium, Seema Joshi, M.K. Tyagi, Mathura Dutt Joshi and Yadav Singh Rawat of L.B.S. National Academy of Administration, Mussoorie, India;

Dr. Anita Srivastava, J. Ramakrishnan and Rachna of National Informatics Centre, National Academy, Mussoorie, India;

Professor Nicholas Stern, Dr. Jeanne Dreze, Dr. Peter Lanjouw, Stephenn Howes, Dr. David Coady and Leila Abericci of STICERD, London School of Economics and Political Science, London, U.K.;

Professor Graham Chapman, Dr. David Taylor and Dr. Peter Robb of School of Oriental and African Studies, London, U.K.;

Professor Richard Ford, Clark University, Worcestor, U.S.A.;

Dr. Robin Sharp of IIED, London, U.K.;

Dr. Bo Gohl of F.S.P., F.A.O., Botswana;

Corrie Sprenkels of Zwenshambee Brigade Trust, Botswana;

Helen McLaren of IDS, Sussex, U.K.;

Dr. Arunish Chawla and Dr. Elan Govan, I.A.S. Probationers, 58th batch, L.B.S. National Academy of Administration, Mussoorie, India;

Somesh Kumar, S.D.M., Bodhan, Nizamabad, Andhra Pradesh, India;

Rekha Tyagi and Sheela Tyagi of Dehradun, India;

Indian Civil Service Probationers, 58th Foundation Course, 56th Foundation course, 55th Foundation course and their corresponding trainees for the IAS Professional Courses, Phase-I, L.B.S. National Academy of Administration, Mussoorie (U.P.), India;

Kamal Kar, Seva Bharati, Kapgari, Midnapore, India;

Md. Shahabuddin, Farookh Bhai, Subrata Chakravarty, Samadbhai, Babu Bhai, Nargis Bano of PROSIKHA, Bangladesh;

Aroma Goon, Rebecca Rodrigues and Rokeiya of Bangladesh;

Anup Pujari, Bangalore, India;

Sumita Roy, Manager, Odhav, Punjab National Bank, Gujarat, India;

M.N.Roy (ex-District Magistrate, Midnapore, West Bengal), R.S.

Shukla (ex-Additional District Magistrate, Midnapore, West Bengal), Arun Mishra (Additional District Magistrate, Midnapore, West Bengal), Mihir Kumar Pahari (Sabhapati, Panchayat Samity, Midnapore, West Bengal) and Pannalal Ghosh, Gram Sewak, Arjuni Mouza, Midnapur, West Bengal;
Madhukar Patil (District Magistrate, Thane), Amitabh Joshi (Additional District Magistrate, Thane), V.R. Adki (B.D.O., District Thane), B.B. Gawali (Tehsildar, Tehsil Murbad, District Thane), Dr. D.C. Bora (Primary Health Centre, Tokawade, District Thane), C.H. Sugandhi (Nayab Tehsildar, District Thane), A.K. Patil (Soil Conservation Supervisor, District Thane), N.K. Yadav (Circle Inspector, District Thane), J.S. Padwal (Tallati, District Thane), R.V. Deshmukh (Tallati, District Thane) and J.H. Bhalla (Gram Sewak, District Thane);
Mitali Sen-Gavai, Director, Integrated Child Development Scheme, Government of Maharashtra, Bombay, and
Sushil Priyadarshee, District Magistrate, Dehradun.

Institutions

My special thanks are to those institutions which provided me with infrastructural support from time time.

The institutions are listed below:

L.B.S. National Academy of Administration, Mussoorie (Uttar Pradesh), India;
London School of Economics and Political Science, London, U.K.;
International Institute for Environment and Development, London, U.K.;
Institute of Development Studies, Sussex, U.K.;
South-Asian Centre, School of Oriental and African Studies, London, U.K.;
Centre for Applied Social Sciences, Harare, Zimbabwe;
Administrative Staff College of India, Hyderabad, India;
Farming Systems Programme, F.A.O., Gabarone, Botswana;
PROSIKHA, Dacca, Bangladesh;
Ford Foundation, Bangladesh;
USEFI, Fulbright House, New Delhi, India;
The British Council, London, U.K.;
United Nations Development Programme, Geneva;

Stanford University, Stanford, U.S.A.;
University of California at Berkeley, California, U.S.A. and
Clark University, Worcestor, U.S.A.

There are a few other names without whom my learning and writing in the area of rural participation would not have surfaced. I express my sincere gratitude to Dr. Robert Chambers of IDS, Sussex for his inspiration, comments and invaluable support in my writings on rural participation.

The professional contributions of Dr. Jules N. Pretty, Dr.John Thompson, Irene Guijt, Dr. Ian Scoones and Deviani Vyas of Sustainable Agriculture Programme of IIED, London are gratefully acknowledged.

I am also thankful to Ashok Mittal of Concept Publishing Co., New Delhi for all the trouble undertaken by him in publication of this book.

My thanks are due to my mother, Indrani Sen Gupta, who provided critical support towards this study by caring for my child during many of my field trips. Last but not the least, I wish to thank my husband Dr. Amitabha Mukherjee for all his comments, advice and help and my son Taponeel who encouraged me to write on rural participation and was so happy to learn about the present work.

NEELA MUKHERJEE

Mussoorie 2nd April, 1993

CONTENTS

CONTENT OF TABLES

LIST OF CHARTS

1

THE LOGIC OF PARTICIPATION AND THE METHODOLOGY OF PARTICIPATORY RURAL APPRAISAL

This chapter begins with a discussion of the conventional approach to rural development and then goes into describing the significance, meaning and principles of Participatory Rural Appraisal (PRA) as a methodology of participatory development. It serves as an introductory chapter to describe the logic of participation in the context of which the other chapters are to be understood and appreciated.

1.1 The Magic Wand of Development

In our search for rural development, we are faced with a plethora of exotic and sophisticated models where we tend to switch between one and the other, improvise them and make them operational. Our exotic models are professionally convenient in suggesting magic formulae for development and generalized programmes for implementation. Take for instance, the Harrod-Domar model which shows that a rise in savings rate is enough to bring about a rise in national income given the capital-output ratio (Todaro:1989). In this model, the whole process and speed of development is compressed into a simplistic solution of raising the savings rate of an economy. Again, in his two-sector model of development, with unlimited supplies of labour, Lewis demonstrates that the surplus labour from the traditional rural sector would be absorbed by the modern sector through re-investment of surplus in the modern sector to augment its capital stock. The above process of modern-sector growth and expansion in employment would continue until all surplus labour from the traditional sector is absorbed by the modern sector (Lewis:1955). And by means of such a structural change the traditional sector would experience the magic of development.

There are a host of other models advocating set formulae for raising national income and attaining development (Todaro:1989). In such models, there are a few variables to monitor such as the savings rate or the investment in modern sector, which are supposed to ensure end-results. Based on such models, our policy-makers, donors, planners and implementators design and implement development programmes. They presuppose people as mere objects of development and adopt a 'blue-print' to the issues concerned whether at the national or at the village level.

1.1.1 *The Illusion of the Magic Wand*

Even when the results from application of such models are not very encouraging, especially in the context of rural development, the mind-set is such that development professionals are unable to accept anything different. They tend to operate on a basic presumption that they are the best judge of any situation and that the welfare of rural masses rests on them. Hence, with best of knowledge, resources and benign motives they remain oblivious of the fact that majority of their rural clienteles are passive spectators of their magic wand of development.

Often, to have a glimpse of rural areas, rural development professionals are quick to organise short field trips to gain impressionistic views of rural conditions in villages generally located near a roadside and at a time when the weather is most congenial. Such rural development tourisms add to complacency by providing 'snapshot' views of 'better-off' villages, successful projects and 'well to do' rural elites (Chambers:1991b). All these act as hindrances in the process of realisation that a large chunk of rural masses remain deprived of the fruits of development. Further, it also hinders a basic understanding that in absence of a participatory framework at the grassroot level, projects for rural masses are ill informed, ill conceived and show little capability of generating benefits which the programmes envisage.

1.2 The Fathomless Gap in Perceptions

There is a sea-gap existing between rural perceptions and perceptions of those development professionals from the 'top' involved in planning and implementation of conventional models of rural development. One way to explain this gap is through differing 'worldviews' of development. Different groups use different models to code, organise and interpret their perceptions (Khon Kaen University:1987). Each group sees something that the other overlooks, misses or simply considers irrelevant and unimportant. The 'top' people base their premises on their 'worldview' of development thereby ignoring the 'worldview' of their clienteles concerned. They assess their needs and priorities on the basis of their perceptions which are generally at variance with rural perceptions. Hence in conventional models of rural development, the beliefs, attitudes and values of the rural people involved remain under-perceived, undervalued and simplified. There is also a tendency at the 'top' to generalise and not notice rural variations by space, time, gender, age and ethnic groups (Chambers:1991a). As already mentioned earlier, the borrowed models tend to standardise problems and their solutions and hence the scope for inducing variations remains limited.

For example, take a certain level of income as a conventional measure of well-being generally used by 'top' people to demarcate poor from non-poor. Such a measure may be quite deficient for atleast four reasons. First, it is difficult to express many rural activities in terms of income including variables which are qualitative. Second, there are inconsistencies which persist between a conventional yardstick such as income and the rural realities. This is due to the differences in its connotation, the qualitative differences in such a yardstick used by those at the 'top' and differences in the degree of precision/vagueness attached to quantitative information by the rural people (Jodha:1989). Third, estimated income may fail to reflect rural communities' perceptions of poverty and well-being, by not accounting for functional relationships and linkages which determine them. Finally, the nature, causes, conditions and solutions to rural poverty vary across households, groups, villages and regions and standard levels of income as measures of poverty and well-being have gross limitations. Income, can be an important determinant of well-being, but it is one amongst several determinants.

Use of standardised concepts and yardsticks for identification of rural realities is generally handicapped by the absence of a framework for capturing the complex linkages of rural livelihoods. Such yardsticks present a partial and a simplistic picture of the problem concerned. Hence, their value for policy formulation must be limited. Such an approach undermines rural people's ability to take a long-term view, and their knowledge, creativity and competence in presenting and analyzing complex information (Chambers:1991a).

1.2.1 *The Communication Gap*

On many occasions the differences in rural people's perceptions and of those at the 'top' are reinforced on account of a communication gap. On one hand, the communication gap arises due to the 'top down' model of development where plans are conceptualised and formulated at the national level and then made to percolate down to the lower levels. The programmes and projects framed at the top are handed down to different tiers of development administration for implementation. In this way, it becomes easier to match the resources and the requirements of the rural people from the 'top'. In such a framework communication with rural people is not required by the system and hence it is not essential. On the other hand, the problem of lack of communication has also to do with the rural clienteles themselves, especially the rural poor. The rural poor shy away from communication and tend to feel inhibited to express their views. The very experience of poverty and their struggle to survive can cripple their urge to participate in the development process. Most of the time they are over-burdened in procuring the basic necessities of life. Often, after long years of deprivation and stagnating conditions, a poor person comes to accept his or her miserable conditions of existence.

1.3 The All-pervasive Questionnaire Survey

The survey method is the conventional method of data collection whether it is a household survey or an agricultural census. The focus of a survey is on general trends and set patterns. It fits well as a methodology of a 'blue-print' for development which on the basis of an average picture can prescribe an uniform package of solutions. The data are collected either through a selected sample or through a complete enumeration of all subjects covered by a survey. The principle governing the method of survey seeks to establish a general law which operates within given conditions. In a survey-questionnaire, the objective is to find a general picture by repeating a set of questions as given in a questionnaire and investigations are carried out on that basis. Data gathered from a survey can provide an average picture of trends and characteristics across time and across regions relating to different aspects.

1.3.1 *The Naivety of Questionnaire Survey*

For study of complex relationships in the rural world a method like survey runs the danger of being elementary and simplistic. The variables determining the complex relationships, their nature and intensity and their process of interactions may not be easily captured through a set of questions to be answered in precise terms and numerical magnitudes.

In a questionnaire survey, people are the objects of enquiry or investigation and are treated as passive entities. They have no involvement in the enquiry going on and cannot influence its sense and direction. The outsiders' understanding of a situation or a phenomenon is considered as objective. The questions are framed by outsiders based on their perceptions of the rural world. In the process of applying pre-set questions and mechanically repeating them from person to person the survey misses out on the scope for eliciting rural people's views and their perspectives.

In the context of a 'top down' approach, data collected through survey can provide an average picture for application of generalized policies and instruments but remains considerably weak in analysis of difference and projecting people's perceptions through participation.

The duration of time involved from designing a questionnaire-survey to publishing its results tends to be a long and elaborate process. As a consequence, much of the information collected through a survey becomes dated and of limited use in framing of policies and programmes. Here the issue involved is in what ways can data collection be improved in terms of both efficiency and time.

1.4 The Dis-illusionment

The fallacies of the presumptions from the 'top' have done enough damage to the pursuit of rural development. Many of the ambitious targets of rural development have been met, yet, a large proportion of rural masses remain in a deplorable condition of existence and the programmes have largely benefited the 'better offs' in rural areas. As empirically evident from the experiences of many developing countries, the conventional approach has consistently failed to answer the phenomena of poverty, unemployment, inequality and ecological degradation. It is being slowly realised that our conventional models are neither realistic nor sustainable in the long run.

In the sphere of agricultural development in particular and rural development, in general, efforts of the conventional or 'production centred' development model was mostly directed to increase the yield of major cereals in resource rich, stable and homogeneous environments. The fruits of Green Revolution got concentrated in the hands of the rich farmers and the problems of resource-poor farmers in diverse and complex environments had deteriorated over the years. The problems of resource-poor farmers, had not been attended to by the strategy of the Green Revolution for the problems and opportunities of poor farmers for development were essentially different.

The dis-illusionment from the conventional approach is growing over the years. It is being increasingly recognised in different quarters that development involves a complex system of inter-relationships between people, socio-economic processes and local environment. It is in this context that the perceptions of the people who experience it are critical in understanding the intricacies of this relationship.

1.5 The Crux of Development

The process of development is a process of transformation of the quality of life of individuals. Development, in short, is an exercise in betterment of quality of life. It focuses on the nature of life which people are able to live. There are certain activities and conditions (like being free from hunger, free from disease) which determine the nature of life. They are the functioning of an individual and well-being is an evaluation of such functioning. There are a multitude of determinants of well-being such as income, access to means of production, access to public goods and services etc. whereas the constituents of well-being are health, welfare, freedom and choice (Sen:1988).

Well-being is a state of being happy and doing well in life, conditions for which are likely to differ from individual to individual. It is possible to define certain criteria which are basic to achievement of the state of well-being for e.g. food security and availability of jobs which contribute to both physical and mental well-being. But it is of great significance as to who defines such criteria and indicators of well-being given the functioning of an individual and the complexities of rural livelihood. If such criteria are defined by outsiders then the question is how relevant are they to the individual concerned.

In the context of rural development and individual well-being, the issue is how rural perceptions can be revealed and understood so as to (a) take account of the indigenous knowledge system, (b) incorporate rural diversity (c) make rural communities involved in pursuit of their own well-being and (d) make professional's task more worthwhile and rewarding in the process of collecting, analyzing and using rural information base for development. The search is on for an appropriate methodology for rural development. The present study is yet another addition in that search process. It presents principles, methods and field level applications in rural participation based on the methodology of Participatory Rural Appraisal (PRA).

1.5.1 *Some Realisations from the 'Top'*

In recent years, indigenous knowledge system constitutes an alternative model for sustainable development. It is the sum total of experience and knowledge of a given group that forms the basis for decision-making in the face of familiar and unfamiliar problems and challenges (Warren and Cashman:1988). It is being gradually appreciated by policy makers, planners, administrators and donor agencies that until and unless the rural people can participate in rural development programmes such programmes administered by outside agencies remain 'exogeneous' to the rural community which can adversely affect the results of such programmes.

One way to narrow the gap is by getting closer to rural people and learning from them. By 'getting closer' is meant establishing better rapport and channels of communications. For this purpose, the attitudes have to be friendly and the conventional methods for knowing them would have to undergo significant changes with the objective of empowering the rural people in their pursuit of a better quality of life.

1.6 The Search for Reality : Emergence of Field-oriented Methods

As a result of the dis-illusionment from the conventional models some efforts were being made in different quarters towards realistic methods, models and approaches. As a result, a multitude of field-oriented methods emerged on the scene. The necessity of disaggregating economic and social data by people and geographical areas was realized so as to highlight the relatively depressed areas and people. New approaches and methods such as Farming Systems Research, Exploratory Survey, Rapid Rural Appraisal and others, whether through observation or through participation, attempted to understand the problems of resource-poor farmers and improve the quality of information collected on them by overcoming the deficiencies of the conventional survey method. These approaches incorporated flexibility of methods and elements of people's participation in different measures in order to reflect field-level realities. As we shall see many of them combined elements of both quantitative and qualitative methods in different proportions.

It is of utmost importance to understand the intricacies of socio-economic and ecological environment within which the resource-poor farmers operate and to resolve their problems by collaborating with them according to their needs and priorities. It was to deal with this issue that the Farming Systems Research (FSR) was evolved in the 60s whose objective was to further research in the area of farming systems, analyse problems and plan research and extension activities. The form of evolution of FSR was different in agricultural institutions located in different countries. However, the common theme in the evolution was a field-oriented and comprehensive approach of a multi-disciplinary team through repeated farm trials with some degree of farmers' participation. FSR, used many traditional methods while innovating new methods to yield quick and realistic results.

A host of field-oriented methods were evolving over time. They were efficient enough to yield the same volume of information or even more, in a short period of time, as compared to the survey method which was time-consuming and involved a lengthy procedure for collection and analysis of data. Such methods from various sources were put together with a different label known as Rapid Rural Appraisal (RRA).

Rapid Rural Appraisal or RRA developed as a methodology in the 1970s, influenced by Farming Systems Research (FSR) and other methods. Some of the early pathbreakers of such methodology were Robert Chambers, Peter Hildebrand, Robert Rhoades and Michael Collinson who along with others met in Conferences at the Institute of Development Studies in October 1978 and December 1979. Through the literature, the concept of RRA spread in different parts of the world and in the mid-eighties there was a wide array of experience from the applications of RRA in different field situations.

As a methodology for agricultural development RRA was developed for quick field-oriented results with objectives as follows:

(i) appraising agricultural and other needs of rural community;

(ii) prioritising areas of research tailored to such needs;
(iii) assessing feasibility of developmental needs and action plans;
(iv) implementing action plans, monitoring and evaluating them.

Rapid Rural Appraisal or RRA is a way of organizing people for collecting and analyzing information within a short time span. It can be defined as any systematic process of investigation to acquire new information in order to draw and validate inferences, hypotheses, observations and conclusions in a limited period of time. It has flexibility to adjust to situations because it does not imply or recommend a standard set of methods to be applied in each case. The methods vary from situation to situation and are determined by local conditions, local problems and objectives at hand.

1.6.1 *Other Field-oriented Methods*

There were other methods evolving alongside RRA and were similar in nature to RRA. These were being developed mostly by the agriculture research centres in different countries. Such methods similar to Rapid Rural Appraisal or Rapid Appraisal (Chambers:1981) are 'Sondeo' (Hildebrand:1981), 'Informal Agricultural Survey' (Rhoades:1982), 'Informal Methods' and 'Reconnaissance Survey' (Shaner et.al:1982), 'Samuhik Brahman' of Nepal (Mathema and Galt:1987); 'Diagnosis and Design' (Raintree and Young:1983) and 'Exploratory Survey' (Collinson:1981).

Some of the important methods are explained below, namely, (i)Informal Agricultural Survey; (ii)Exploratory Survey; (iii)Sondeo; (d)Agroecosystem Analysis; and (iv)Rapid Agro-Ecosystem Zoning.

The Exploratory Survey (Collinson:1981) or the CIMMYT methodology has three stages: (i) a standard questionnaire used for zoning of target population groups into recommendation domains; (ii) semi-structured interviews for an exploratory survey of target group of farmers and (iii) for verification through a formal survey of a large number of farmers in the target area based on a questionnaire developed from the exploratory survey. CIMMYT has used the above stages in the field of agricultural development to analyse how better management techniques are affected by resource requirements.

Informal Agricultural Survey (Rhoades:1979) was developed at the International Potato Center(CIP). This is similar to stages (i) and (ii) of CIMMYT's methodology except that the questionnaire is not used, instead other methods like ranking of problems and transect walk are used. CIP provides a basis for (i) designing and conducting of formal survey for deeper investigation; (ii) assessing feasibility of projects in selected regions; and (iii) taking up specific problems of farms for experimentation.

Agroecological zones (Hildebrand:1981) are identified on the basis of similarity of conditions within zones and farmers within the zone are supposed to have similar set of problems and technological needs. Two simple techniques for facilitating agroecological zones are agroecological transects and field plotting. Field plotting is to plot a field in terms of its crop associations and observed farming practices, while, agroecological transect by a team involves walking from lower to higher (or higher to lower) elevations. Notes are taken of natural vegetation, land-use and sketches of field shapes and crops grown. Technological features of agricultural practices are taken into account including factors like settlement patterns, distance between fields, factors determining labour or time requirements in getting to fields or transporting the harvest to market (Rhoades:1987).

"Sondeo" was developed by Hildebrand for multi-disciplinary work at ICTA in Guatemala. It was used to familiarise staff with area in which they work and to identify innovation which can be tried directly with the farmers. The method can be adapted for other purposes such as natural resource appraisal, health, nutrition and social and economic change. "Sondeo" is an exercise consisting broadly of the following steps. The first is to identify an homogeneous cropping system amongst many farmers in the area; two teams of agricultural scientists and social scientists are taken to the area for a week or so, who combine in smaller teams of two each to work and exchange experience. Inter-disciplinary teams of small size work in the site for a few days and keep sharing their experiences, changing team members and deciding on priorities. This is followed by a report written over the week-end by different team members. The team scientists working on agricultural technology use the information by "Sondeo" to make their research more field-oriented.

Agroecosystem Analysis (Conway:1985, 1986) is concerned with the agroecosystem of an area whose micro unit is generally the village. Agroecosystem represents a system comprising of a set of natural conditions (climate, topography, soil etc.) and a set of agricultural activity existing to utilize that system. In an agroecosystem analysis a secondary data review precedes the field visit where a set of diagrams are produced on the agroecosystem based on direct observation, semi-structured interviews and other visual methods of

RRA. The diagrams produced through fields visits are then analysed, on the basis of which a list is made of important factors influencing the agroecosystem in terms of productivity, stability, sustainability and equity. It also gives rise to a set of key questions and related hypotheses which the group agrees to be important. This is followed by an assessment of impact of innovations and interventions on system properties and their prioritisation through ranking. The key questions are both research and development questions where the first category leads to further research while the second category leads to development action (McCracken, Pretty and Conway:1988).

The methodology of Rapid Agroecosystem Zoning (Conway et. al.:1987) consists of treating areas in terms of General Recommendation Domains (GRDs) to help in development planning. GRDs consists of individual domains or areas characterised by similar biophysical and socio-economic features on the basis of which appropriate recommendations are made regarding innovations and interventions.

The field-oriented methods have some features in common such as (i) quicker than conventional methods; (ii) applied in field situations; (iii) learning directly from people; (iv) semi-structured, multi-disciplinary approach with flexibility and innovation; and (v) emphasis on understanding processes through involving people, gathering insights on problems and their probable solution rather than final answers and recommendations (Conway:1988). However, RRA and similar methods remain 'extractive' i.e. researchers observing, writing and analysing. The field-oriented methods leave much scope for inducing greater element of participation.

1.7 The Transition to Participation

The requirement of the shifting paradigm of development was not only a relatively quicker method of data collection but also one which would help local people to perform their own analysis. Hence, certain elements were required to be incorporated in RRA and other field-oriented methods to make them participatory and more broad-based in terms of their applications. It was a shift of emphasis from 'rapid' or 'quick' to 'participatory' and 'empowering' which fitted well with a participatory approach to rural development and became the starting point of PRA. The origin of PRA as a methodology can be traced back to the multitude of methods and approaches which gradually emerged since the seventies mainly due to unsatisfactory results obtained from application of the conventional methodology to rural development.

In a short period of time, PRA as a methodology has gained in strength through its emphasis on 'participation' in line with the paradigmatic shift which is slowly taking place and has helped to fill the vacuum existing in the sphere of rural development. This has also made for its quick spread.

1.8 **Participatory Rural Appraisal**

Participatory Rural Appraisal (PRA) is a methodology for interacting with villagers, understanding them and learning from them. It involves a set of principles, a process of communication and a menu of methods for seeking villagers' participation in putting forward their points of view about any issue and enabling them do their own analysis with a view to make use of such learning. It initiates a participatory process and sustains it. Its principles and the menu of methods help in organizing participation.

PRA is a means of collecting different kinds of data, identifying and mobilising intended groups and evoking their participation and also opening ways in which intended groups can participate in decision-making, project design, execution and monitoring. It provides an alternative framework for data collection and analysis. Because of its participatory nature, it is an useful methodology to focus attention on people, their livelihoods and their inter-relationships with socio-economic and ecological factors.

PRA constitutes a process of involvement with rural people for indigenous knowledge-building exercises. It is a way of learning from and with villagers to investigate, analyse and evaluate constraints and opportunities. It helps to make informed and timely decisions regarding development projects. The participation of rural people can be facilitated through PRA for planning, implementing and monitoring of rural development programmes.

PRA is sometimes known as Participatory Rapid Appraisal where the emphasis is on both 'participatory' and 'rapid'. The emphasis on 'rapid' however, is more in terms of data collection and less in terms of the process of development or even implementation of plans. Other names are also used for describing PRA, some of which are Participatory Rapid Rural Appraisal (PRRA) and Participatory Learning Method (PALM). PRA, as practised in the field has given rise to different schools of PRA with difference in style and emphasis

(Chambers:1991b).

The use of PRA lies in pursuing selected objectives through application of its principles, processes and methods. PRA sessions can be conducted with different objectives in view or there can be a mix of objectives to serve. Some of the objectives are as given below:

(i) for greater and better involvement of villagers by learning about their perceptions, experiences and capabilities;
(ii) to generate information and collection of data for immediate or future use;
(iii) for learning about the impacts of earlier or on-going policies and programmes and to frame new ones;
(iv) for estimating trends and ascertaining conditions of the issues at hand;
(v) for validation or cross-checking of data collected from other sources;
(vi) for training of different categories of persons involved, in the development process, whether from the government, NGOs, banks, donor agencies, researchers, extension agents, scientists etc.; and
(vii) for research studies on use of PRA and to suggest improvements in its methodology.

PRA is a process of participation with the villagers in which rapport-building paves the way for them to perform their own analysis and to express themselves whether by means of 'verbals' like narration or 'visuals' such as making a map. The final product of PRA would differ in output and content depending on several factors. The content is in terms of how the process is established and what methods are used and how the analysis progresses. Sometimes an exercise in PRA may not yield the desired results in spite of best efforts. Or it may involve long durations before anything fruitful happens. Hence, the output of PRA cannot be predicted with any degree of certainty. Sometimes more time is required and better efforts and newer ways can make things happen.

1.8.1 *Principles of PRA*

The principles guiding PRA are discussed below:

(i) Optimal Ignorance

In order to minimise cost and time, the principle of optimal ignorance is applied by the facilitators which means knowing what is worth knowing and knowing enough to serve the purpose and not knowing the rest or not trying to find out more. Associated with this is seeking appropriate imprecision or avoiding precision that is not necessary (Chambers:1992).

(ii) Seeking Diversity

PRA is concerned more with analysis of difference rather than looking for representativeness of results or data collected. It is looking for diverse rural events, different processes and forces explaining various relationships in rural communities.

(iii) Offsetting Biases and Triangulating

PRA is essentially a methodology to offset biases of rural development tourism (RDT) and the survey method. It aims at offsetting such biases by being relaxed and not rushing, listening and not lecturing, probing and not speeding indifferently and looking for participation of rural poor and other weaker sections of rural communities (Chambers:1992).

The process of triangulating is an important part of PRA. For any data generated it is essential to check the reliability and validity of the data by putting them to different tests. Triangulation is cross-checking the data in different ways. This is done through use of various methods and by using different sources to validate information. 'Triangulation' is adopted as a principle to improve accuracy. It involves conscious, non-random selection in different dimensions such as (a) team composition, (b) units of observation and (c) PRA methods. Team composition is generally inter-disciplinary and can be constituted in such a manner so as to have the information generated from different perspectives. The units of observation can be changed in order to cross check the information gained and one has the option of going for deeper probing if necessary. Many different groups can be used in combination so as to arrive at views from different angles. Other sources of information such as secondary data sources can also be used. Again, different PRA methods can be used to test and verify a piece of information. For e.g., semi-structured interviews can be supplemented by farm maps, livelihood analysis and flow charts.

(iv) Listening and Learning, Learning Rapidly and Progressively and Learning through Participation

Knowledge of rural people constitutes the base for the socio-economic and agro-ecological information. They have their experiences, their history and culture, their ideas, their priorities and preferences. Listening to rural people helps them in portraying their points of view which otherwise remain unknown. The greater the interaction with rural people in the capacity of a listener rather than a speaker, the greater is the learning achieved. The amount of learning can increase progressively with participation of those who form the subject of enquiry.

These principles make for different features of PRA, some of which are that learning is iterative, methods are innovative and interactive and the process of PRA remains informal so as to facilitate participation.

1.8.2 *The Foundations of PRA — Behaviour/Attitudes, Methods and. Sharing*

There are three basic foundations of PRA. These are: (i) attitudes and behaviour, (ii) methods and (iii) sharing which together determine the nature of PRA. Each of these is incomplete without the other. Since PRA is essentially in a participatory mode, the attitudes and behaviour required are those which are favourable to participation. There are certain kinds of attitudes/behaviour which are not conducive to participation. The attitude of an outsider as a 'giver' of benefits to the rural masses or the behaviour of that of a 'privileged' outsider with an poor villager can act as a major stumbling block in communication. Without an appropriate mode of behaviour the rural masses can feel left out and be withdrawn and not wish to express themselves. Much of such an exercise can be a lost one.

In this section we shall discuss two foundations of PRA namely attitudes and behaviour and the aspect of sharing. The other foundation of PRA as reflected in the methods are explained in Chapter 2.

(i) Congenial Attitudes and Behaviour

Generally an outsider's entry in a village raises questions and curiosity in the minds of the villagers. Hence the behaviour of the outsider is essential in removing doubts and in building rapport with the villagers. The behaviour of an outsider as a listener and a learner together with the quality of embracing errors, if any, reflect the true spirit of PRA. Friendly behaviour can have several advantages. It can help the outsider to gain entry or have acceptance in a village community. However, some kinds of behaviour can make for distortion of impressions of the villagers and can discourage them from expressing their opinions or can even distort the information required.

Not only are the behaviour and attitudes of listening, learning and having respect for rural people are important but also non-verbal behaviour such as the body language is expected to be in tune with the attitudes and behaviours and should reflect correct signals indicating respect, concern and a serious intention to learn from the villagers.

Some of the beliefs and attitudes which can form a basis for appropriate behaviour so as to elicit participation are as follows:

(a) any knowledge and experience should be respected;
(b) rural people generally have a storehouse of indigenous technical knowledge and experience which can be of great use;
(c) the rural people are entitled to have knowledge about rural development programmes, to express their views and to participate in their effective implementation;
(d) the outsider has an opportunity of learning from the rural people about rural life;
(e) the rural people are capable of rational decision-making, implementing, monitoring and evaluating it whether as a community, a group, a household or as individuals.

(ii) Mutual Sharing

Direct people's participation is a basic element of PRA. Without such participation, PRA is not feasible, for the outsider is not able to know and understand the systems within which the rural people operate. The outsider can guess, make hunches, try to impute his/her knowledge and values and attribute qualifications in order to understand rural conditions and processes. But an outsider's understanding tends to be much inferior from the one who actually experiences it. Whether it is participation by a community/communities, groups or individuals, the greater the participation the better is the quality of information generated through PRA.

On the one hand, it is important that a villager is willing to participate and share his/her perceptions and problems and, on the other hand, it is equally desirable that the outsider also has the necessary attitudes and communicating skills to evoke the necessary participation from the other side. If a person is not willing to participate then either he/she does it of his/her own choice or he/she does not find the behaviour of the outsider congenial and a PRA may not be possible. Hence willingness of rural people to share their knowledge and experience and their problems and priorities is equally important.

A PRA experience in a remote tribal village named Thippapur, (Andhra Pradesh) in India became a difficult exercise with the villagers unwilling to participate. The outsiders made gestures to appear friendly yet the villagers were not receptive to them. The villagers were not only apathetic but appeared hostile to the outsiders. Only after repeated attempts to speak to the villagers did the atmosphere slowly become friendly. Repetition of friendly gestures helped in rapport-building which gradually brought more and more villagers to interact with the outsiders. (Kumar Somesh and Kumari Santhi:1991).

The attributes required in the outsiders are respect for the local people, patience and skills of listening and if these attributes are not reflected in the behaviour of the person conducting PRA then it can become a difficult exercise. The right kind of behaviour facilitates the application of PRA methods. Behaviour can influence the degree of participation and application of the methods. Opportunities for PRA can be conducted with better results when the behaviour is congenial to it. On different occasions, during PRA sessions, villagers may not be willing to participate beyond a point for reasons such as tiredness, fatigue or jobs at hand. If stretched beyond such a point a PRA session can become quite unproductive.

1.8.3 *The kinds of PRA*

PRA can be of different kinds, namely, (a) exploratory, (b) topical, (c) deductive, (d) research, training and statistics, (e) planning and implementing and (f) monitoring and evaluative.

(a) Exploratory PRA

A PRA exercise can be undertaken for understanding broad patterns and trends in a rural society. Such exploratory PRAs are quite common to reveal different aspects of rural life and also suggest important issues to be pursued. It can form a basis for further probing into selected areas which appear important and useful. A theme for further analysis can emerge out of such exploration which can help in undertaking either a PRA exercise or help in framing a survey questionnaire on realistic lines.

(b) Topical PRA

This has to do with a particular topic which either constitutes the area of investigation by the outsiders or has been suggested by the villagers as a key area to be focused. For instance, in a theme like 'seasonality' of rural life, PRA can help in exploring different dimensions of the theme under consideration. An exploratory PRA helps in placing the topic in the relevant context. Different hypotheses can be formulated regarding investigation of a topic and can be probed by means of different methods. Or an enquiry through PRA can take its own course without formulation of any specific hypothesis on the issue. A topic can be probed across different groups in a village, across gender, caste, age etc., as a community and over time. Its objective is to generate as much information as possible on a selected topic. It is intensive in its approach and can help in analysis of a particular topic at great length.

(c) Deductive PRA

A PRA exercise can be conducted on different aspects of village life which can then provide a basis for having information on themes not directly attempted through PRA. This can help in relating different aspects of the problem to other factors and also help in dealing with sensitive issues. Deductive PRA is especially helpful when used for themes which require tact and cannot be directly probed on account of the nature of the subject concerned such as communal tensions, class struggles, corruption etc. There can be some topics, which are efficiently treated through relating them with different aspects of village life rather than treating them through direct probing. For instance, to learn about the impact of local corruption in a village, direct questions on corruption may not yield much response. PRA sessions on different aspects of village life related to corruption would give indications of it extent and impact.

(d) PRA for Research and Training and Statistics

PRAs can be for the purpose of researching in the forms of participation, its processes and methods. PRA can be of a training type for training of different groups of professionals who are likely to use them in their fieldwork or for further training.

(e) PRA for Planning and Implementation

PRA can be conducted for designing projects and implementing them. All stages of a project cycle can be based on PRAs. It can make projects more adaptable to local needs. If village communities or groups are involved in a project right from its initiation, the chances of sustainability of the project increases through people's participation. As shown by experience, if a project is exogenously set up in a village, the chances of success of that project is low. The risk bearing inclination of the beneficiaries is expected to be higher in all cases where the local people or the intended beneficiaries participate in choosing the projects.

(f) Monitoring and Evaluative PRA

PRA can form a basis for monitoring and evaluation of projects and programmes. It can touch upon the problems faced by the community/groups/households in running of projects. With identification of problems, operation of projects can be better informed and solutions to avoid or resolve those problems can be sought through PRA. A 'before and after' comparison of projects can be undertaken for projects which have either involved PRA methods in project formulation and appraisal or those which have not used them at all. In the former case, it becomes easier for the monitoring process to identify the gaps between expected and actual results and improving the working of the project as far as practicable while in the latter case monitoring PRA can bring to light several aspects and areas not considered earlier or taken into account while designing the project and in its implementation. However, PRA methods can attempt to provide an opportunity to rectify the defects of the earlier project planning and can suggest scope for possible improvement within the framework of project management.

For monitoring by PRA methods there can be a set of indicators proposed indigenously to guide effective implementation of projects. In case of problematic situations, monitoring through PRA can bring different groups in the villages together for conflict resolution along with other officials such as planners, implementators and other facilitators associated with the programme. Different kinds of impacts of the project such as socio-economic, ecological, and other short-term and long-term impacts can be examined and analysed by the villagers and outside team for the purpose of monitoring. The flexibility in PRA methods would add to the flexibility in monitoring so as to work towards improving the performance of the project and in the process minimise the adverse consequences.

Summary

In this chapter, we have discussed the flaws in the conventional 'blue-print' models of development, the gap in perceptions of those at the 'top' and the rural people and the communication gap between the two. The problems of the conventional method of questionnaire survey has also been reflected upon. Later, in this chapter, we have presented the major attempts at different quarters of development to move towards realistic approaches and methods so as to have better understanding of rural realities. The chapter also traces the significance of participatory development and in this context discusses the principles, foundations and other details of the methodology of Participatory Rural Appraisal.

REFERENCES

Chambers, Robert (1981), 'Rapid Rural Appraisal: Rationale and Repertoire', *IDS Discussion Paper* No.155, IDS, Sussex.

Chambers, Robert (1991a), 'In Search of Professionalism, Bureaucracy and Sustainable Livelihoods for the 21st Century', typescript, IDS, Sussex, 28th May.

Chambers, Robert (1991b). 'Shortcut and Participatory Methods for Gaining Social Information for Projects, in Cernea, Michael M. (ed.), *Putting People First, Sociological Variables in Rural Development*, World Bank, Oxford University Press.

Chambers, Robert (1992), Rural Appraisal: Rapid, Relaxed and Participatory, *Discussion Paper* No. 311, Institute of Development Studies, October, Sussex.

Conway, G.R. (1985), Agroecosystem Analysis, *Agricultural Administration*, 20 (1), 31.

Conway, G.R.(1986), *Agroecosystem Analysis for Research and Development*, Winrock International Institute for Agricultural Development, Bangkok, Thailand.

Conway, G.R., Mian A., Alam Z., Yar M., and Husain T. (1987), Agroecosystem Zoning of the Hunza Valley: First Iteration - May 1987, Draft Report, International Institute for Environment and Development, London.

Conway, Gordon (1988),'Editorial — What's in a name', *RRA Notes* No.1, June.

Collinson, M.P.(1981), 'The Exploratory Survey Content, Methods and Detailed Guidelines, for Discussions with farmers', in *CIMMYT Eastern Africa Economic*

Programme Farming Systems Newsletter, April-June.

Hildebrand, P.E.(1981), Combining Disciplines in Rapid Appraisal: The Sondeo Approach, *Agricultural Administration* 8 (6), 423.

Jodha, N.S. (1989), 'Social Science Research on Rural Change: Some Gaps', in Bardhan Pranab, (ed.), *Conversations Between Economists and Anthropologists,* Oxford University Press, Oxford.

Kumar, Somesh and Kumari, Santhi A., "The Thippapur Experience: A PRA Diary", *RRA Notes*, No. 11, December, 1991.

Lewis, W. Arthur (1955), *The Theory of Economic Growth*, Homewood, Richard D. Irwin, Illinois.

Khon Kaen University (1987), Proceedings of 1985 International Conference on Rapid Rural Appraisal, Rural Systems Research and Farming Systems Research Projects, Khon Kaen University, Khon Kaen, Thailand.

Mathema, S.B. and Galt, D.L. (1987), 'The Samuhik Brahman Process in Nepal: A Multidisciplinary Group Activity to Approach Farmers', Paper presented at the Workshop on Farmers and Agricultural Research: Complementary Methods, Institute of Development Studies, England 26-31 July.

Raintree, J.B. and Young, A. (1983), *Guidelines for Agroforestry Diagnosis and Design*, ICRAF Working Paper no.6, Nairobi.

Rhoades, R.E. (1982), *The Art of the Informal Agricultural Survey*, International Potato Centre, Lima.

Rhoades, Robert E. (1987), 'Basic Field Techniques for Rapid Rural Appraisal', Proceedings of 1985 International Conference on Rapid Rural Appraisal, Rural Systems Research and Farming Systems Research Projects, Khon Kaen University, Khon Kaen, Thailand.

McCracken, Jennifer, Pretty, Jules and Conway, Gordon (1988), *An Introduction to Rapid Rural Appraisal*, Sustainable Agriculture Department, I.I.E.D., London.

Sen, Amartya (1988), 'The Concept of Development' in Chenery H.B. and Srinivasan T.N. (ed.), *Handbook of Development Economics*, volume I, North Holland.

Shaner, W.W., Philipp, P.F. and Schmehl, W.R.(1982), *Farming Systems Research and Development: Guidelines for Developing Countries*, Westview Press, Boulder, Colorado.

Todaro, Michael P. (1989), *Economic Development in the Third World*, Longman, New York.

Warren, Michael D. and Cashman, Kristin (1989), *Indigenous Knowledge for Sustainable Agriculture and Rural Development*, Gatekeeper Series no. SA 10, Sustainable Agriculture programme, IIED, London.

2

PARTICIPATORY METHODS AND RURAL KNOWLEDGE

In this chapter, we describe the indigenous knowledge sources and the different methods of PRA. Each method is illustrated with a real life application. The first section of the chapter summarizes different rural sources for indigenous knowledge. The second section has a discussion on the importance of visual methods followed by a description of different PRA methods and a note on sequencing of such methods.

The innovative nature of PRA has helped in adding a large number of methods to its inventory. Such methods have provided rural people with an opportunity to express themselves and have been instrumental in exposing various dimensions of their living which normally remain unperceived or under-perceived. There are different aspects of rural life not all of which can be expressed in quantitative magnitudes. Some of them can be quantified while others are better described qualitatively while some others remain hidden and elusive. Many aspects of rural life can be best expressed through ranking and relative comparisons, for example, ranking of households on the basis of wealth and well-being analysis. Some aspects of rural life can also be sensitive and a direct approach to such issues can be a frustrating experience. A relative ranking and scoring of selected issues can enable relative comparisons without directly going into absolute measurements.

2.1 Indigenous Knowledge and Its Sources

Before discussing the methods it is important to identify the indigenous knowledge sources which are available in rural areas. These sources are a rich repertoire of culture, practices, beliefs and approaches for understanding and appreciating rural people. Learning about rural knowledge base from different sources can be an important aspect of a PRA exercise. It can help to set the context of views expressed by rural people. Much of it is embodied in the art, history and culture of the place concerned. There may or may not exist books to read on local culture and practices but they can be better appreciated through other media of expression such as local art, culture, dance, drama, etc. Some of the sources of rural knowledge base are described below:

(i) *Local Histories*: Local histories, whether found in research reports and books or narrated by villagers can provide background materials and insights for cultural perceptions. These can highlight socio-economic basis and the evolution of legal basis of land ownership and common property resources to explain local people's way of life. Oral history as narrated by rural people cannot only be rich in content but can also serve other purposes for a fieldworker. It can be used for dating and putting ages to people as required by different studies, for instance, nutritional studies. It can also be used in trying to put a time scale on local vegetation change and can form an excellent way to break the ice with local people in order to initiate discussion on different topics (Mearns:1988).

(ii) *Stories, Profiles, Case Studies and Portraits*: These are anecdotal evidences and other real-life experiences narrated by rural people describing different incidents and happenings in the area concerned. They are generally oral when recounted by the villager and they can help in depicting the conditions of livelihood, the major historical events and the coping strategies of the rural people. A study conducted in a village in North West Pakistan describes how portraits and stories provided colourful descriptions recounted by the local people. These portraits and stories helped to bring to life the conditions of the local people which appeared difficult to be expressed through visual modes (Pretty:1988).

(iii) *Folk-Lore, Folk Tales, Proverbs and Poetry*: Each locality, tribe or community can have its literary and artistic materials which can contain a considerable amount of information depicting its local culture, the legends, the rituals, the legendary characters and practices. One can know them from the local people and have them explained. These can depict the conditions, the beliefs, the problems, the perceptions, and the traditions of the community or tribe concerned. They can also form a basis to learn and interpret the current conditions in light of a community's culture and traditions.

(iv) *Sharing Practices and Beliefs*: Sharing of practices and beliefs of villagers with outsiders can improve the level of interaction and can help in de-mystifying village practices and beliefs to the outsiders. The history of beliefs and practices of a community and their rationale, if any, can also be unravelled through group interactions. Table 2.1 provides an illustration of such practices and beliefs.

TABLE 2.1: Indigenous Practices and Beliefs in Meenakshipuram village in Kamarajar District, Tamil Nadu, India

The following indigenous practices and beliefs were found from the discussions held with the farmers of Meenakshipuram village by a PRA team. These practices were helping to increase and sustain crop production and in treatment of some common ailments:

* Crushed *neem* seed extract used for spraying cotton as a pest control mechanism.
* Goat pellet powder mixed with seeds and sown to improve germination.
* Pesticide use has eradicated *striga* - a parasitic weed on pearl millet.
* Coriander sown in late *karthegai* (November) escapes from dew injury and yields more.
* Application of tank silt is very good for crops. It is used to cover manure pits.
* Tying snails shell around neck prevents abortion in goats.
* Sheep penning brings more wealth.
* Goats are primarily kept as economic buffer. They are sold during summer months when the income is low.
* Sorghum fencing: if sorghum is grown in thick stand around cotton fields it saves cotton.
* Growing blackgram in an intercrop is better for the next crop compared with green gram.

Source: Vijayraghavan R., Subramanian S.R., Pretty Jules N., and John K.C. (eds.), (1992), *Participatory Rural Appraisal for Agricultural Research at Arupukotai, Tamil Nadu,* Department of Agricultural Economics, Centre for Agricultural and Rural Development Studies, Tamil Nadu Agricultural University, Coimbatore and IIED, London.

(v) *Traditional Management Systems, Farming practices and Local Resource Inventory*: In order to know more about the background of a village, its traditional management system and local resource inventory can act as sources generating information about the local people, their conditions, their knowledge-systems, their perceptions of local resources and their way of resolving problems through their knowledge and management capabilities.

(vi) Village analysts or key informants can be found amongst the more knowledgeable persons in a village who can help in analysis of information and in raising issues for further probing. The current issues and problem-areas can be summarised by a village analyst and his or her views can be sought from time to time. However, the reliability and validity of such views can be cross-checked with those of others. There can also exists village organisations of different kinds which can be approached for gaining further insights into the issues concerned.

2.2 The PRA Methods

There is perhaps no end to discovery of participatory methods. With each problem there tends to be an appropriate form of expression, appropriate to explain a particular issue concerned. It also depends on the user who uses a particular method or methods to express himself or herself. PRA methods can be broadly sub-divided into (i) methods (indirectly or directly) supportive of PRA and (ii) methods which involve direct participation of the villagers. In category (i), normally the outsider is active in data generation and collection with little or no involvement of the villager concerned. While in category (ii) the villagers are involved right from the beginning and it is they who perform their own analysis and generate data.

The use of different methods mainly depends on the ways of expression which the villagers wish to adopt. The methods aid in participation and expression of views. Much depends on the relevance of the issue and the way in which the villagers wish to present it, their convenience of expression as well as their skills. The methods that can be used on different occasions will be different. Several methods can be combined in different ways in order to analyse issues at hand and conduct an appraisal of the subject under consideration. Some major methods have been described below along with illustrations taken from field situations.

2.2.1 *Methods Supportive of PRA*

PRA looks for support from different kinds of methods and uses both primary and secondary data review for gaining knowledge of rural situations apart from learning through direct participation. The method of direct observation can also be supportive of the learning process in a PRA exercise.

(a) Primary and Secondary Data Review

Before conducting a PRA exercise it is often possible to get some background information on the area to be covered. Such information can help in describing broad features and trends of the area concerned, covering different aspects at different points of time. Sources of such data can be both primary and secondary. The primary source constitutes materials gathered first hand and have a direct relationship with people, situations or events that are being studied such as court records, letters, minutes, memoranda, notes and diaries. They cannot be viewed uncritically which means one has to combine other materials and sources along with the primary sources (Burgess:1990).

Secondary sources of data can be found in published materials which may include transcript or summaries of primary source materials. Some secondary sources are surveys, books, reports, plans, official records, census records, project reports, maps, aerial photographs, journalistic articles, newspaper cuttings, research papers and data files from computers. The organizations and individuals who are usually associated with collecting such data are government, researchers, statistical agencies, local level educational and technical institutions, non-government organizations, donor agencies, remote-sensing agencies etc. These are generally data collected through the conventional methods and one needs to keep in mind the limitations of such sources, the ways in which materials have been selected, analysed and presented. For use of all kinds of documentary evidence it is important to guard against problems concerning authenticity, availability, sampling, interpretation and presentation. Documentary evidence provides data link up with other data obtained through field research (Burgess:1990).

One of the important secondary sources is aerial photography which can help to know more about the physical features of a certain area. They provide a visual medium to farmers to locate their land and other resources on the ground and explain them (Sandford:1989). They reduce spatial biases which most field workers tend to encounter on the ground. Experience shows that farmers are quite comfortable with interpreting aerial photographs (Dewees:1989). Two main field uses of aerial photographs are as aids for mapping boundaries of land and as a focus point for discussion in interviews (Mearns:1989).

It is worthwhile to mention in this context, that the conventional methods support PRA and can also help in evaluation of PRA.

(b) Direct Observation

An outsider as a facilitator can directly observe an activity in a village and also observe the effort, skill or knowledge involved in it and can have a first hand appreciation of the activity in question. This helps in forming preliminary ideas about activities or processes observed from close quarters. It is better than guess-work or forming such ideas from a distance or from a remote official headquarters. However, direct observation by itself is generally not enough. It has to be supplemented by other methods of PRA to make it participatory and in the process to enrich the information generated.

2.2.2 *Methods with Direct Participation*

There are different PRA methods involving direct participation, many of which include diagrams as an integral part. The importance of diagrams is explained below:

Importance of Diagramming: Diagrams help in building consensus and can form a base for resolving conflicts and difference of opinions. They help in cross-checking of information and building up of knowledge on that basis (RRA Notes:1991). Any discussion is enriched by visual diagrams. They present greater details than what verbal discussions usually are capable of. They help in discussion of related issues important to different villagers, both literate and illiterate. They make the villagers feel interested and involved in discussing different aspects of their own village. They can be more objective than verbal group discussions since any changes to be incorporated in them can take place immediately and any error made can be rectified at once.

It also facilitates exchange of views on the basis of information presented in maps and diagrams. The maps are open for group discussions especially for those who do not have an opportunity to mention their points for discussion and be able to present their views in case of verbal discussions. In case of diagrams, people have the entire set for discussion in front of them and can go into finer details without missing any important point.

Maps can be made with great ease anywhere and they help the

outsider to have a visual impression of the issue under discussion. On many occasions, maps help in rapport-building exercises and in comparison of different views, cultural perceptions and changes over time. They reveal perceptions and preferences which are otherwise hidden and obscure. They form bases for data generation, planning, implementation, monitoring and evaluation.

The use of diagrams, however, have some limitations. Some diagrams drawn are too complicated to be widely understood. This can be avoided through appropriate notes taken as and when diagrams are being explained by the villagers. Sometimes it may become difficult to explain all parts of a diagram due to lack of space. The scope of diagram is limited in case of large gatherings (McCracken:1989). Diagrams drawn on the ground using local materials, unless translated into paper or photographed, can be easily damaged and destroyed.

The major PRA methods involving direct participation are explained below.

(a) Semi-Structured Interviews

Semi-structured interviews are partly structured and mostly unstructured depending on the responses of the person or group with whom the interview takes place. It is conducted in an informal manner in a relaxed setting where queries emerge according to the responses received. It is a combination of the outsiders initiating interviews followed by discussions of rural people on the topic concerned. The villagers bring in different aspects related to the question. The interviewer being free to probe, frames subsequent questions according to the aspect concerned. The questions are required to be open-ended. Hence the interview can start with a few pre-set questions and further questioning would depend on the answers received. The interviewer generally has a mental checklist. This helps in maintaining a broad framework for the enquiry and for the flow of queries to be an orderly exercise with the progress of the semi-structured interview. Some important aspects of semi-structured interviews are discussed below.

There can be sequencing and a chain of semi-structured interviews. Different methods of PRA can be combined and sequenced such that information on the problems at hand, their causes and the required policy actions can emerge from a PRA exercise. Semi-structured interviews can be repeated as and when required. After presentation of visual diagrams verbal interactions become necessary for explaining the diagrams. Sequencing of semi-structured interviews with other PRA methods (which is discussed in a later section) help in filling gaps, refreshing memories and communicating one's point of view.

Semi-structured interviews can be conducted with different groups in a village or a community. This is one of the forms of group interviews. Apart from meeting casual groups in villages there are permanent groups based on common interests and activities. Permanent groups can be community groups such as those of small farmers or landless labourers, groups of specialist individuals such as rural artisans or silk weavers; and structured groups, involving a mix of individuals according to ages, wealth, caste and religion (McCracken, Pretty and Conway:1988). Outsiders can meet different groups separately or together to know of their problems and opportunities through semi-structured interviews and other methods.

There can be key probes through semi-structured interviews. Probing is continuing to investigate areas perceived as key issues in a PRA exercise. A semi-structured interview can be followed by probing into areas which the villagers perceive as important. Such probing can be through a combination of both visual and verbal methods.

Semi-structured interviews conducted for an evaluation-exercise of Integrated Rural Development Programme, a poverty alleviation programme brought to fore a critical point in loan repayment by beneficiaries. This evaluation was conducted in a few villages in the districts of Hooghly, Midnapore and Purulia in the State of West Bengal, India, for households owning income generating assets through an official credit-subsidy programme. Many of these households had a poor track record on loan repayment, amongst other problems.

The beneficiaries while discussing their problems expressed their views on problems of loan repayment. They pointed out that most of their assets were such that these generated daily income such as bullock/camel carts, rickshaws, selling vegetables, eggs and other commodities whereas there was no official provision for repayment of loans on a daily/weekly basis, in bits and pieces. Hence, even when they were willing to pay off their loans in tiny amounts they were unable to do so at the end of the day due to lack of arrangements for daily repayments. They were unable to save enough money for future repayments for various reasons. The beneficiaries preferred arrangements for loan repayments which would suit their repaying ability and time. This was an 'eye opener' for the outsiders who were under the impression that either beneficiaries' loan repaying abilities were poor or they were defaulters out of choice. The semi-structured interviews showed the individual problems of loan repayments which the beneficiaries were facing in an organizational set up which could hardly perceive the capabilities and problems of a poor person.

Concurrent surveys conducted to evaluate the programme indicated the number of loan defaultors, the average period after which they defaulted and the different reasons for default (such as loss of income-generating asset, sale of assets and others). The survey results, however, did not reflect the mismatch between the beneficiaries' convenience and ability to repay as indicated above and the official payment arrangements made by the banks.

(b) Do-It-Yourself (DIY)

The activities of rural people can be appreciated better if an outsider who wishes to understand rural realities does them himself or herself. Generally, it appears that such activities involve simple skills of rural people but can be difficult in actual practice. Do-it-yourself gives practical ideas of the complexities involved in rural activities. This can also help in rapport-building with the villagers. For instance, one can plough a field and have a first hand experience of the activities of a farmer or accompany a rural woman to collect fuelwood or fodder and appreciate the difficulties involved in such jobs. Such participation of outsiders in rural activities can often constitute a first step in rapport-building.

(c) Maps and Models

Participatory mapping is crucial to PRA and can be on different aspects of rural life such as social issues, resource, health, wealth, literacy, census, livestock, economic activity, social stratification, forms of livelihood etc. Such maps can portray the image of dwellings in a village, of farms and fields, water collections, forests, soils and of many other aspects depending on the topic under consideration. In participatory mapping and modelling, villagers prepare the map/model of their village with chalks, colours and other materials either on ground or on paper.

It is a rich tool and is commonly used in PRA. It has enormous potential. Maps by villagers provide a basis for knowing different aspects of a village, for instance, the location of dwellings and buildings and land-use patterns as indicated by a social map showing the position of households in a village and their socio-economic characteristics. A village resource map can also show different kinds of natural resources and micro environments. In a resource map, the villagers draw the resource profile of the village depicting different kinds of soils, rivers, ponds, trees, crops and micro environments. The problems can be described and discussed on the basis of a resource map along with the opportunities and the constraints. This can also form a basis for a transect walk to be undertaken from a selected point in the village to another or a walk in selected areas of the village. A resource map combined with a social map is shown in Chart 1.

Once a social map is made by the villagers it becomes easy for them to describe locations within the village in terms of roads and rivers, the characteristics and conditions of the households, the ownership of dwellings and buildings and land-use patterns. In terms of poor and non-poor households in the villages, social maps visually present the location of such households and their key features. In addition, there is also scope for presenting other kinds of information regarding households such as the heads of households whether a female or a male, the dependency ratios, ownership of assets, cattle, beneficiaries under state programmes, health characteristics and so on.

The social map in Chart 2 shows literacy for each household of village Krishna Rakshit Chak of Midnapore district, West Bengal, India. The map illustrates the position of households regarding literacy and shows that some of them have a combination of both literates and illiterates. Such maps can have a direct bearing on adult literacy programmes.

In any village, social maps form an useful basis for identifying problems in different households, their strengths and characteristics. For example, a social map can form an excellent base for a health map indicating the health problems in different households. Maps can be followed by semi-structured interviews.

Models are an advancement over mapping and represent three-dimensional figures, therefore adding height differences in the landscape. They can be made with local materials. Models are useful for land-use planning and watershed planning, for which the problems, treatment and opportunities can be shown on the model itself. A model or a map can also be historical (representing past shape

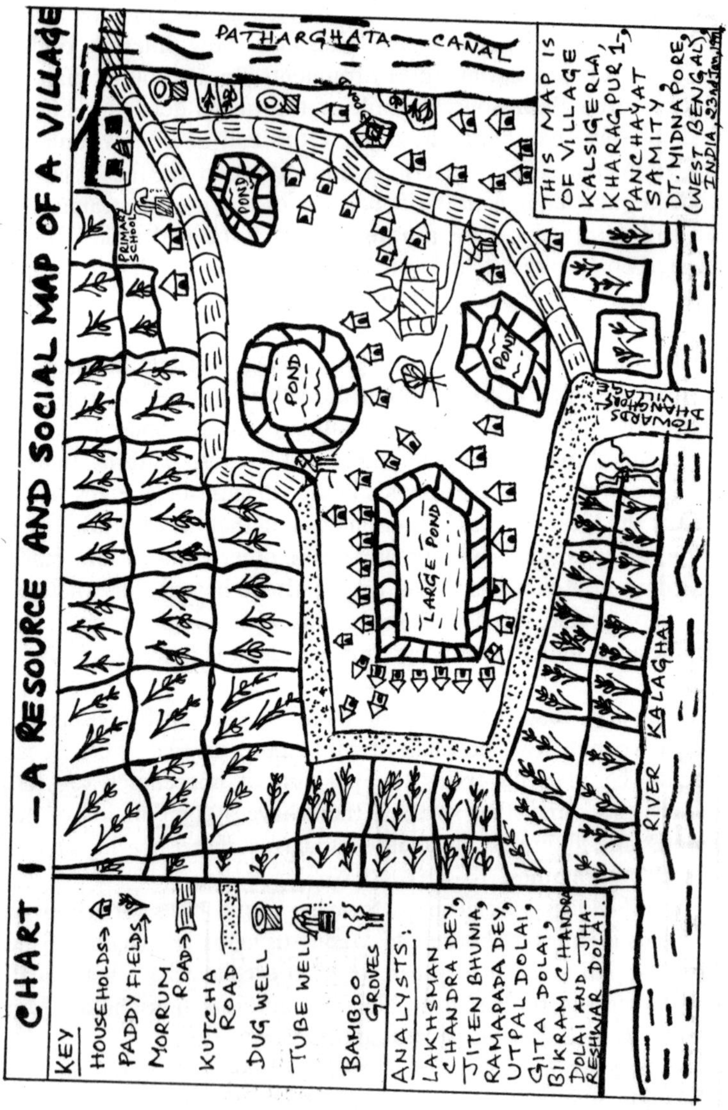
CHART 1 — A RESOURCE AND SOCIAL MAP OF A VILLAGE
KEY
HOUSEHOLDS
PADDY FIELDS
MORRUM ROAD
KUTCHA ROAD
DUG WELL
TUBE WELL
BAMBOO GROVES
ANALYSTS:
LAKHSHMAN CHANDRA DEY, JITEN BHUNIA, RAMAPADA DEY, UTPAL DOLAI, GITA DOLAI, BIKRAM CHANDRA DOLAI AND JHARESHWAR DOLAI.
PATHARGHATA CANAL
THIS MAP IS OF VILLAGE KALSIGERIA, KHARAGPUR 1, PANCHAYAT SAMITY, DT. MIDNAPORE, (WEST BENGAL) INDIA
PRIMARY SCHOOL
POND
POND
POND
LARGE POND
TOWARDS DHANGHORI VILLAGE
RIVER KALAGHAI

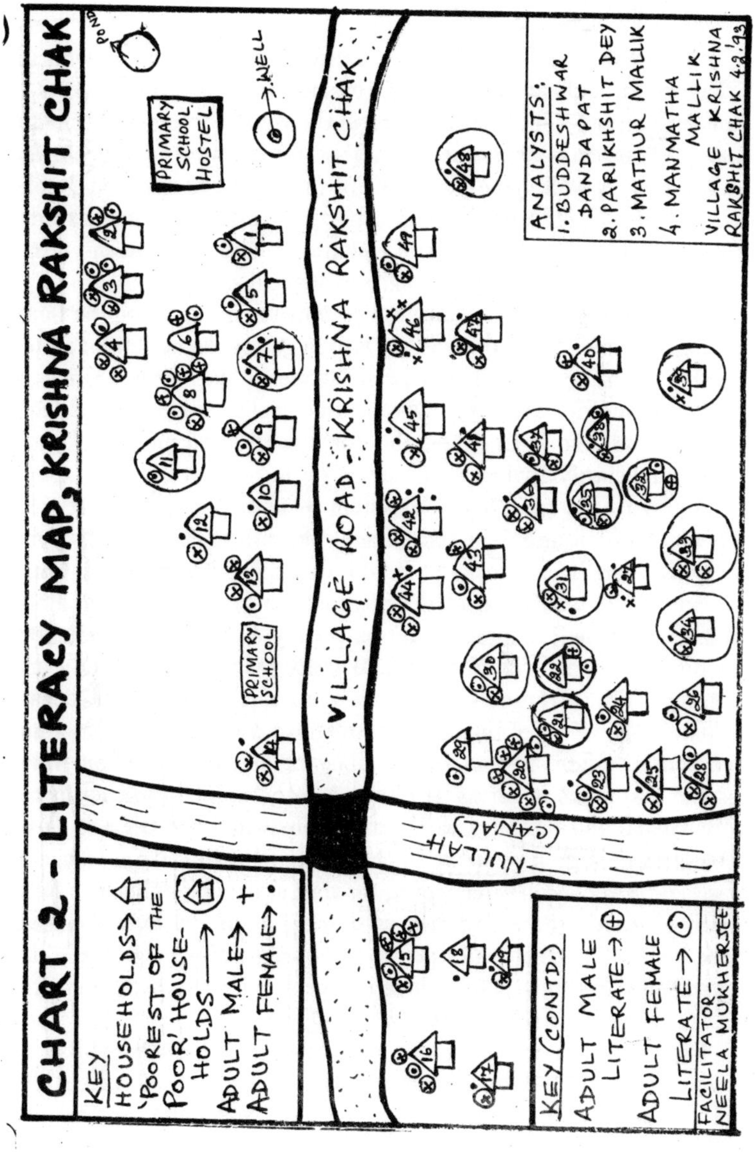
CHART 2 - LITERACY MAP, KRISHNA RAKSHIT CHAK
KEY
HOUSEHOLDS →
'POOREST OF THE POOR' HOUSE-HOLDS →
ADULT MALE → +
ADULT FEMALE → •
KEY (CONTD.)
ADULT MALE LITERATE →
ADULT FEMALE LITERATE →
FACILITATOR- NEELA MUKHERJEE
NULLAH (CANAL)
VILLAGE ROAD - KRISHNA RAKSHIT CHAK
PRIMARY SCHOOL
PRIMARY SCHOOL HOSTEL
WELL
POND
ANALYSTS:
1. BUDDESHWAR DANDAPAT
2. PARIKHSHIT DEY
3. MATHUR MALLIK
4. MANMATHA MALLIK
VILLAGE KRISHNA RAKSHIT CHAK 4.2.'93

or form), current or futuristic (showing future shape of a village or area)(Mascarenhas and Kumar:1991).

(d) **Transect Walk**

Participatory transect walks systematically involve walking with the villagers through an area and discussing about different aspects of land-use and agro-ecological zones in the village observed during the walk. A transect walk is a useful method for knowing rural ecological conditions. A walk from one point of the village to another enables the outsider to observe different aspects of rural ecology and to discuss with rural people about soil conditions, land-use patterns, crops, livestock, micro environments, agro-ecological zones etc.

The importance of a transect lies not only in knowing the agro-ecological zones in rural areas but also in getting an in-depth account from the participating villagers of such zones in the village, their uses, problems and opportunities. One transect walk can be supplemented by other walks so as to enable the outsider to learn more about any village and clarify doubts.

As far as the rural agro-ecosystem of poor people is concerned, the physical variations in the village, the micro-environments and their use can be appreciated better through transect walks which provide visual exposition of the physical features of a village along with local people's interpretations. They help to overcome the 'roadside' bias associated with field visits (McCracken, Pretty and Conway:1988). Transects help a team to carry out a detailed participatory appraisal of the agroecosystem of a village or an area under consideration. It can reveal villagers' perceptions about their natural resources in terms of either a resource-rich or a resource-poor village and the intra-variations in physical resources and agro-ecological conditions existing in the village. However, if a village is large and has considerable variations then it may be difficult to have a full grasp of the village through a single or multiple transect walk/walks. Transect walks across major agro-ecological zones can nevertheless be undertaken which can prove effective in conjunction with drawing of a resource map by the villagers.

The transect shown in Chart 3 is a village of Sidra Kordofan in Sudan. It describes different features of the area covered such as the soil conditions, the landuse, the crops and vegetation grown, the problems and the opportunities. A set of problems have been stated for each agro-ecological zone as described in the transect. The opportunities identified are also in accordance with the zones and

CHART 3

TRANSECT

VILLAGE OF SIDRA KORDOFAN, SUDAN

SOIL	rocky	gravel	gravel	sand	clay
LANDUSE	forest	farmland village	village	farmland grazing	farmland
CROPS AND VEGETATION	trees, bamboo	grass, shrubs, millet, sesame		sesame, beans, hibiscus	sorghum, ground-nuts
PROBLEMS	erosion	drought, pests		drought, pests, low soil fertility	drought
OPPORTUNITIES	fuelwood, timber, bamboo	pasture, rainfed farming	market transport, water, credit, health-care, school	pasture, rainfed farming	flood-recession farming

SOURCE: THEIS JOACHIM AND GRADY HEATHER M., (1991), PARTICIPATORY RAPID APPRAISAL FOR COMMUNITY DEVELOPMENT, A TRAINING MANUAL BASED ON EXPERIENCES IN THE MIDDLE EAST AND NORTH AFRICA, I.I.E.D. AND SAVE THE CHILDREN FEDERATION, LONDON.

different policy actions have been suggested which can be undertaken for the area concerned.

(e) **Seasonal Diagramming**

Rural livelihoods are integrally connected with seasonality. Each season has its own problems and the rural people have different strategies for their livelihoods. The seasons bear heavily on the physical conditions which in turn influence their lives. Seasons bring about differences in climatic conditions, in crops grown, in availability of water, food, fuel and fodder which in turn influence the living conditions in rural areas. Seasonal diagramming can lead to comparisons of related aspects of rural livelihoods such as seasonal variations and their linkages with food, employment, work load, disease etc.

Different aspects of rural life can be reflected through seasonal diagramming. A method which reflects the 'seasonality' aspect of rural livelihood is a much better method than a picture presented by some other method such as a questionnaire survey taken at two different points of a year. In the latter case, the 'seasonality' factor can either be neutralised through 'averaging' or conclusions can be drawn on the basis of a partial picture for one season.

In seasonal diagramming, the villagers prepare diagrams and charts (either with chalks or other materials) either on ground or on paper, of various socio-economic and physical phenomena such as seasonal wages received, food consumed, prices, crops grown, rainfall patterns, sickness and others. In such diagramming, the villagers can make diagrams for seasons/months/days showing the rainfall pattern, employment, labour activity, labour availability, food availability, food intake, disease, fodder, fuelwood availability, livestock disease, need for credit, credit availability and many other aspects.

Chart 4 presents a seasonal calendar of peasants in North Kordofan, Sudan which starts from the month of May. It shows the days of rainfall, crops growing on sand and clay, seasonal labour demand, allied activities like gum tapping, water sources, labour migration and seasonal variations in price of sorghum (Theis and Grady: 1991).

Chart 5 is a seasonal analysis of nine diseases in Udaanampatti village in India. It shows seasonal frequency of diseases of which for e.g., headache is a frequently occurring disease while the frequency of diarrhoea is largely concentrated in the months of April, October and November. The chart can be directly linked to policy measures in terms of strengthening of primary health care depending on the frequency of a disease and its period concerned.

CHART 4

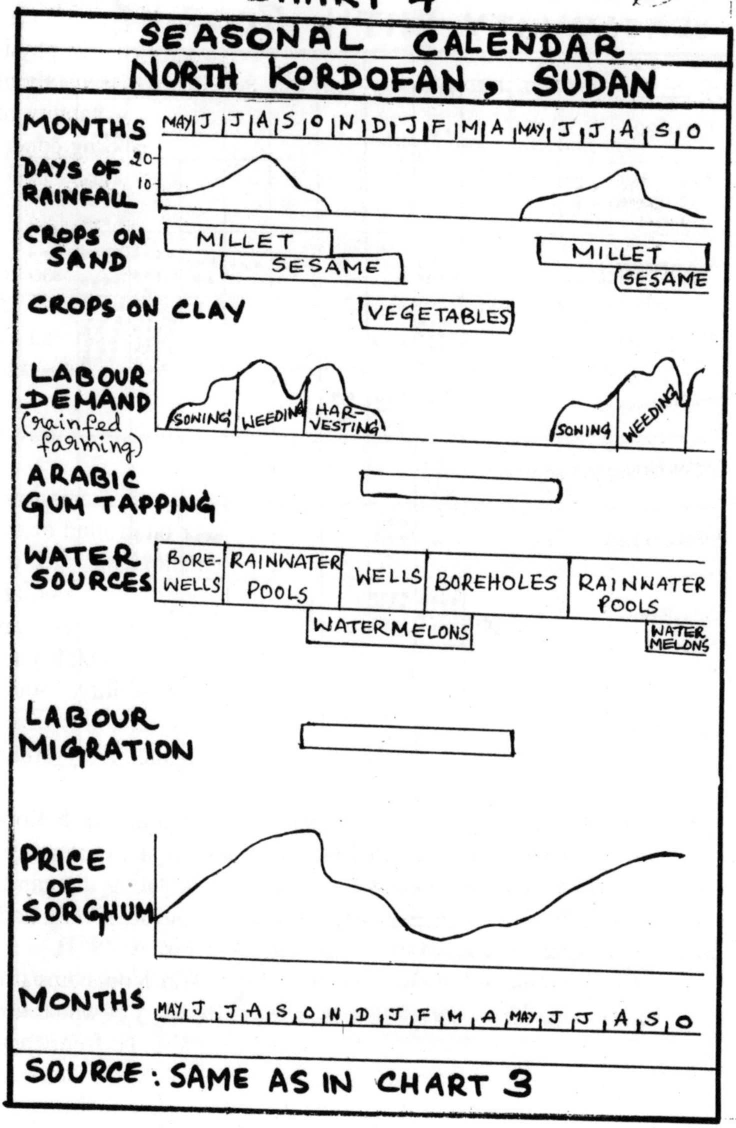
SEASONAL CALENDAR
NORTH KORDOFAN, SUDAN
MONTHS
MAY J J A S O N D J F M A MAY J J A S O
DAYS OF RAINFALL
20
10
CROPS ON SAND
MILLET
SESAME
MILLET
SESAME
CROPS ON CLAY
VEGETABLES
LABOUR DEMAND (rainfed farming)
SOWING
WEEDING
HAR-VESTING
SOWING
WEEDING
ARABIC GUM TAPPING
WATER SOURCES
BORE-WELLS
RAINWATER POOLS
WELLS
BOREHOLES
RAINWATER POOLS
WATERMELONS
WATER MELONS
LABOUR MIGRATION
PRICE OF SORGHUM
MONTHS
MAY J J A S O N D J F M A MAY J J A S O
SOURCE: SAME AS IN CHART 3

CHART 5

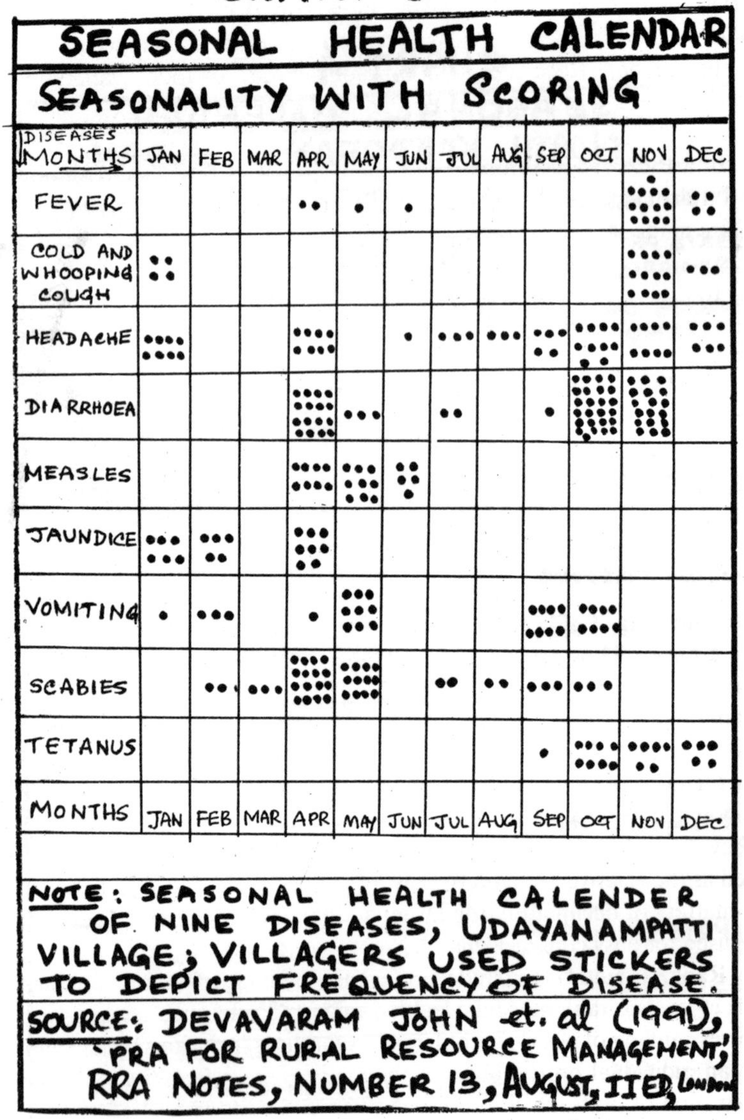
SEASONAL HEALTH CALENDAR
SEASONALITY WITH SCORING
DISEASES
MONTHS
JAN FEB MAR APR MAY JUN JUL AUG SEP OCT NOV DEC
FEVER
COLD AND WHOOPING COUGH
HEADACHE
DIARRHOEA
MEASLES
JAUNDICE
VOMITING
SCABIES
TETANUS
MONTHS
NOTE: SEASONAL HEALTH CALENDER OF NINE DISEASES, UDAYANAMPATTI VILLAGE; VILLAGERS USED STICKERS TO DEPICT FREQUENCY OF DISEASE.
SOURCE: DEVAVARAM JOHN et. al (1991), 'PRA FOR RURAL RESOURCE MANAGEMENT,' RRA NOTES, NUMBER 13, AUGUST, IIED, LONDON

Food Calendar

Food calendar is a specific use of seasonal diagramming. Seasonal variations in food availability is an integral part of rural life and the PRA method of food calendar can illustrate food availability in different seasons. Both the quantum and the kind of food availability over different seasons or months can be shown through a food calendar.

In a PRA session in Nlaphwane village which is a resource-poor and a drought-affected village near Francistown, Botswana, the villagers made a food calendar as shown in Chart 6 and explained their seasonal food availability in a normal year. They drew a food calendar to describe the availability of food stocks, their staple food in different months and how they supplement it with other kinds of food. They started with the month of July in a normal year with adequate rainfall when they indicated that after the harvest they have 30 bags of staple food. The food availability dwindles slowly over different months and reaches seven bags in June after completion of a full year. It is supplemented through a wide variety of food from the 'wild' and other sources.

(f) **Ranking and Scoring**

The methods of ranking and scoring reveal priorities and preferences. They provide opportunities to rural people to physically rank and re-rank some items or preferences or some uses and explain their reasons for a given ranking. Matrix ranking and scoring is most appropriate when outsiders wish to obtain precise information on relationships amongst several different criteria and wish to rank only a few alternatives, related to uses, preferences or priorities. They can help in understanding rural people's criteria for ranking as well as the relative position of their priorities, preferences and choice in matters of occupation, food, fuel, fodder, energy-use etc. They can be used for easy comparisons.

Ranking methods include preference ranking, pairwise ranking, direct matrix ranking and wealth ranking. Preference ranking involves ranking of a set of problems/preferences/priorities by a group or an individual on the basis of their criteria or perceptions. An illustration of preference ranking is given in Chart 7 which shows the relative preference for three kinds of cotton varieties with ten criteria. At the end of the matrix, the last row shows that the overall rating is in favour of the third variety of cotton.

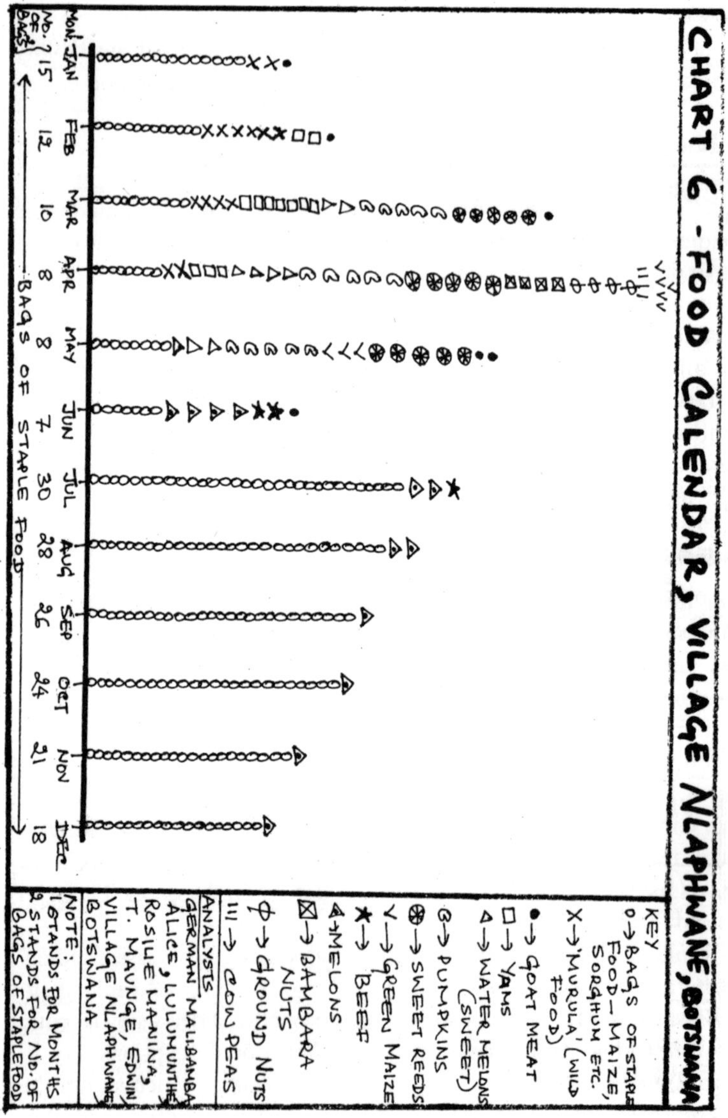
CHART 6 - FOOD CALENDAR, VILLAGE NLAPHWANE, BOTSWANA
MON. JAN FEB MAR APR MAY JUN JUL AUG SEP OCT NOV DEC
NO. OF BAGS 15 12 10 8 8 7 30 28 26 24 21 18
BAGS OF STAPLE FOOD
KEY
O → BAGS OF STAPLE FOOD – MAIZE, SORGHUM ETC.
X → 'MURULA' (WILD FOOD)
● → GOAT MEAT
□ → YAMS
Δ → WATER MELONS (SWEET)
ᘏ → PUMPKINS
⊛ → SWEET REEDS
V → GREEN MAIZE
★ → BEEF
Δ → MELONS
⊠ → BAMBARA NUTS
ф → GROUND NUTS
III → COW PEAS
ANALYSTS
GERMAN MALIBAMBA, ALICE, LULUMUNTHE, ROSILIE MANINA, T. MAUNGE, EDWIN
VILLAGE NLAPHWANE, BOTSWANA
NOTE:
1 STANDS FOR MONTHS
2 STANDS FOR No. OF BAGS OF STAPLE FOOD

CHART 7

MATRIX RANKING OF COTTON VARIETIES

CRITERIA \ VARIETIES	COTTON VARIETIES		
	KARUNGANNI	LAKSHMI	LRA 5166
DURATION	×××××××	×××××	××××
BOLLS/PLANTS	[illegible]	××××××××××	×××××××××××××××××××××
BOLL WEIGHT	×××	×××××	××××××××××
PEST RESISTANCE	×××××	×	××
RESPONSE TO MANURING	××	×××	×××××
EASE OF BOLL PICKING	×	×××	×××××
POSSIBILITY OF INTERCROPPING	×	×	×××
PESTICIDE USE	–	×	×××
YIELD	×	××	××××
NET RETURN	×	×××	××××
OVERALL RATING	③	②	①

PARTICIPANT – MR. PAI PANDIAN, VILLAGE-MEENAKSHIPURAM, THE SIGN × INDICATES SCORING.

<u>SOURCE:</u> SAME AS IN TABLE 2.1, CHAPTER 2.

Pairwise Ranking

Pairwise ranking which uses two items or attributes at a time for ranking can be used to explore rural people's criteria for choosing one alternative over another. A villager or a group of villagers can compare one pair at a time and give reasons for the choice made. At the end, the most favoured choice is identified if it is a question of choice or, the major problem is identified in case of problems being ranked.

Matrix Scoring

In a matrix scoring exercise, different attributes and criteria are listed which are ranked either on the basis of fixed scoring (say scoring out of ten) or free scoring (as many or as less as one wishes) according to their relative importance. An exercise in matrix scoring can illustrate its use in revealing perceptions of rural people.

An exercise on wild trees was conducted in Nlaphwane village in Botswana. The scores are presented in Chart 8. In the matrix scoring exercise, 16 wild trees along with their 16 uses were identified and score for each tree was placed in the matrix, according to its relative use. The villagers used seeds for free scoring. For instance, it can be observed from the matrix that 'Mupani' tree had the following uses (i) firewood, (ii) poles for making houses, (iii) fencing fields, (iv) fibres (v) edible fruits and worms, (vi) shade, (vii) animal fodder and (vii) less harmful insects. Each of these uses had a separate score according to their importance to the villagers.

The exercise of matrix scoring of trees provides a wealth of information. It shows how wild trees play a significant role in the lives of rural people. It also shows how the relative utility of each tree is different to the villagers. The rural people are conversant with such uses because they use them in their daily lives.

(g) Wealth Ranking and Grouping

Wealth ranking/grouping is a method of ranking/grouping of households on the basis of income, wealth and other local measures of well-being. Different criteria can be used for wealth ranking/grouping based on rural perceptions. Wealth ranking/grouping is based on the presumption that rural people have the necessary knowledge to rank/group households which implies that they have knowledge of kinds and position of household assets, other items and attributes of the households concerned.

CHART 8 – MATRIX SCORING

MATRIX SCORING OF WILD TREES, VILLAGE NLAPHWANE, BOTSWANA

CRITERIA FOR SCORING	1 MUPANI	2 MOSO	3 MOROJA	4 MURULA	5 MIZE	6 MBOLA	7 NSUNU	8 MUMU	9 MBGETI	10 MPAWA	11 SWANJA	12 NTAMBA	13 NKWAKWA	14 NTHUNU	15 SKESE	16 MPANDA
1. FIREWOOD	20	4	2		1	2	1		12					3	12	
2. POLES FOR HOUSING	7				12	8	11		11							
3. FENCING FIELDS	9				5	4	5									
4. FENCING WELLS		10							8							
5. FENCING CATTLE																
6. 'DASHIBOMA'					10			8	8							
7. FIBRE-MAKING	10														17	
8. SQUEEZING BEER								15								
9. EDIBLE	9		12	8				13		13	10	9	10			
10. SHADE	7		6	10				8		7					8	9
11. TO STRAIGHTEN WELLS									9					8		
12. TO GRIND SEEDS				12												
13. MAKING OF YOLKS						13	9								13	17
14. MEDICINES				14	6						13					
15. LESS HARMFUL INSECTS	18	12	11	13						13	10	8	9		11	13
16. ANIMAL FODDER	5	4		5		4	3	3		5		5	7	5	4	5

Grandin's (1988) method of card-sorting is a method for wealth ranking where a list of households is prepared with each household having a separate number. The number of each household together with the name of the head of the household are written on separate pieces of paper which are then ranked by some key informants individually according to their criteria. The different criteria used in ranking by key informants emerges from their discussion on wealth classification which also helps in cross checking of the list and the final wealth classes are computed on that basis. Direct probing of wealth of any household is a sensitive topic. This method helps in ranking of households without any discussion of absolute wealth of the households concerned. Wealth ranking helps in understanding socio-economic disparities amongst households and reveals local criteria for wealth classification. It helps in stratification of a sample according to people's criteria for further study and policy-making. It also helps in examining survey data from a rural perspective (Scoones:1988).

One other way of wealth ranking/grouping is that of wealth mapping which can also be used to generate information on well-being of different households or members of a community through comparison of households by different criteria of rural people. In a social map, wealth of different households can be identified by key informants, separately or together, and on that basis, they can be ranked one after another or formed into different groups. This can illustrate the socio-economic disparities within a village according to rural people's criteria. An interesting aspect of wealth mapping is that the points of distinction between households which outsiders' tend to overlook or miss can form an important basis for differentiating between households and their ranking/grouping by rural people (Mukherjee:1992). As an illustration shown in Chart 9, wealth mapping has been presented as done by villagers in a village named Berapal in Sadar block of Midnapore district in West Bengal, India. The village consists mostly of small and marginal cultivators and landless labourers.

On the basis of the village map, the villagers attempted to group the households. They marked the households which were at the lowest strata of poverty according to their perceptions. These included the widowed households which had single widows as heads of households and were maintaining livelihoods with practically no assets, no regular source of income and not enough to eat throughout the year. Others in this group included agricultural labourers having neither any land, nor any regular source of income or food.

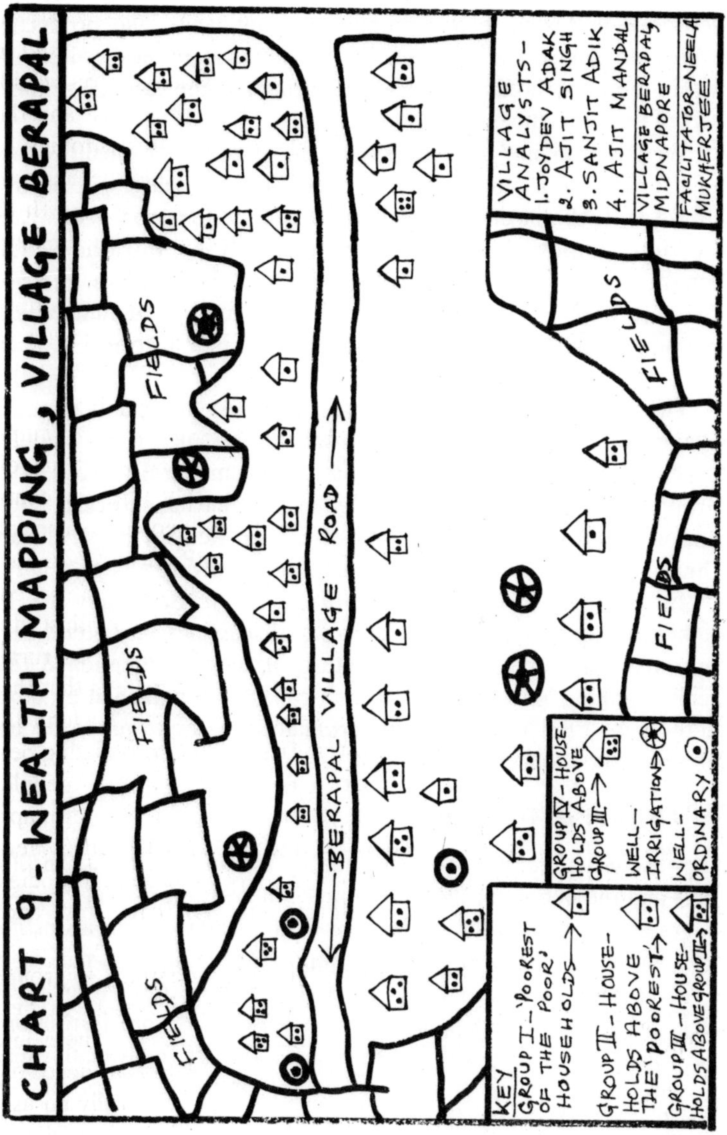
CHART 9 - WEALTH MAPPING, VILLAGE BERAPAL
FIELDS
FIELDS
FIELDS
FIELDS
FIELDS
FIELDS
BERAPAL VILLAGE ROAD
VILLAGE ANALYSTS—
1. JOYDEV ADAK
2. AJIT SINGH
3. SANJIT ADIK
4. AJIT MANDAL
VILLAGE BERADAL, MIDNAPORE
FACILITATOR-NEELA MUKHERJEE
KEY
GROUP I - 'POOREST OF THE POOR' HOUSEHOLDS
GROUP II - HOUSEHOLDS ABOVE THE 'POOREST'
GROUP III - HOUSEHOLDS ABOVE GROUP II
GROUP IV - HOUSEHOLDS ABOVE GROUP III
WELL - IRRIGATION
WELL - ORDINARY

Identification of 'poorest of the poor' households was followed by the villagers marking the groups of households above the extreme poor group. They distinguished between these groups on the basis of land ownership. The group of households next identified was described as having better production from land. The production from land helped them in meeting their consumption requirements within the households as well as procuring income through selling a part of their produce.

Wealth ranking/grouping shows the patterns of wealth across households in a community as per local people's perspective. However, such patterns may tell us little about the process of wealth creation, impoverishment and differentiation. Intra-household dynamics are also not fully reflected in such a method (Scoones:1992). This, however can be overcome by extending wealth mapping to show intra-household differences in a historical perspective.

The method of wealth ranking/grouping becomes cumbersome in villages with large number of households because it may not be feasible to have knowledge about each and every household. Grouping/ranking of households by analysts having sufficient information on all households is also not easy to find for large villages. The same is the case with wealth mapping involving a large number of households. The households are neither easy to be ranked/grouped nor efficient for group discussions on criteria used for ranking/grouping. In this context, it may be mentioned that wealth ranking/grouping by villagers can be strengthened by other methods of PRA such as livelihood analysis so as to probe deeper into the issues concerned.

(h) 'Chappati' or Venn Diagrams

They are visual methods to represent the role of individuals/ institutions and the degree of their importance in decision-making. In such diagrams circles of different size represent an individual or an institution, whose size shows its degree of importance in decision-making in a village and the over-lapping of circles indicate their over-lap in decision-making. Overlapping of circles arise due to one institution/ individual interacting with another institution or individual. Such overlaps may be large or small depending on the extent of interaction. If the circles are separate, the institutions have no contact and if they touch each other there is information passing between institutions.

Venn diagrams can be useful in study of relationships of institutions/individuals with rural people. For rural people in a village community venn diagrams would reflect the kind of communication between them and the rest of the village community and other governmental organizations and NGOs. Different aspects of their life can be taken up to see their interaction and their role in decision-making involving village planning, in running of projects, in distribution of land, credit, water and other assets and in construction of roads, school building, dams etc. Chart 10 shows the key institutions and individuals important for decision-making for control of village water use in Sudan. It identifies the degree of contact and overlap between them in terms of decision-making.

(i) Farm Map

Coming to individual households, a villager with his/her own farm can be asked to draw a map of his/her farm in order to show what he/she grows on his farm and where he/she grows them. Chart 11 is a farm map of a farmer in a village in Botswana. It shows the different crops grown on the field together with the layout of the house on the farm. Chart 12 shows a farm profile of a farmer in a village in India which apart from different crops grown also indicates the soil conditions of the farm. The farm map is an ideal tool for knowing the minute details of a farm, its soil conditions, the variations, different crops grown, water management, fertiliser use, yields and ownership. A farm map can help in sequencing of seasonal analysis or livelihood analysis to know more about livelihood patterns of resource-poor farmers.

(j) Case Study

A case study is a focused study and can be undertaken either for an individual/household/group/community in relation to one or more events or a phenomenon or alternatively, it can be a study of some socio-economic or political change in relation to an individual, household, group or a community. The difference between the traditional case study method and the case study method of PRA is that in the latter case it is essentially based on a participatory mode along with the principles of PRA as discussed earlier. Case study method can be used effectively for analysing coping strategies of rural households during say a famine, drought or a disaster.

CHART 10

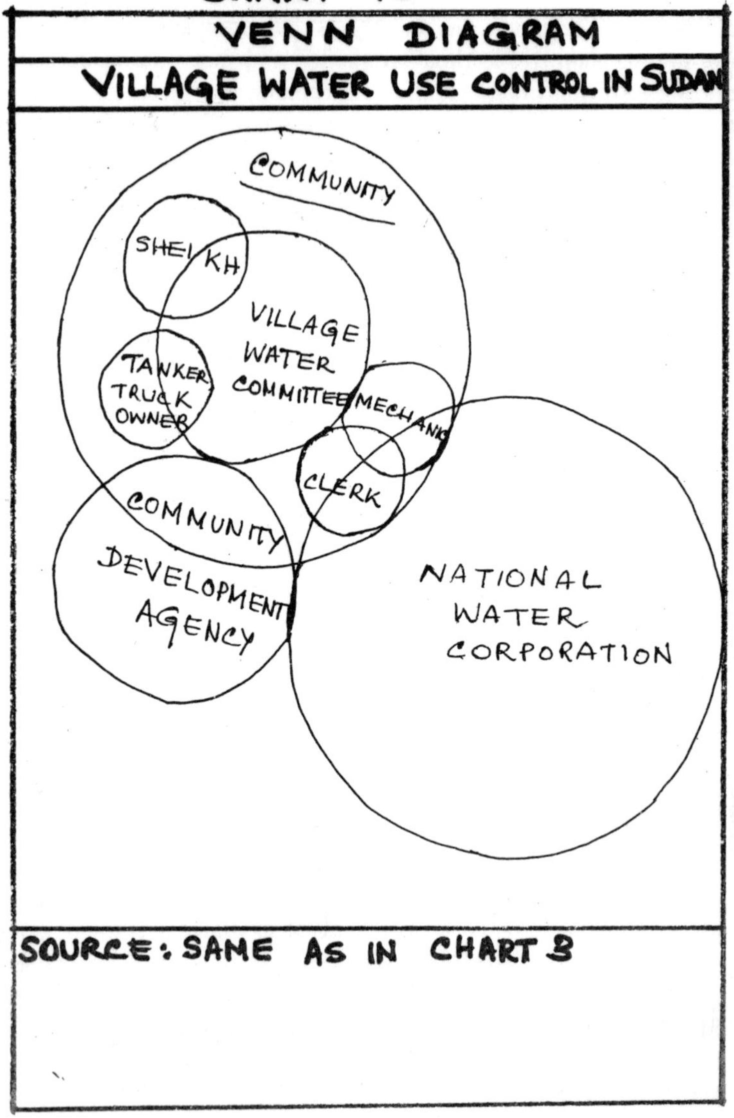
VENN DIAGRAM
VILLAGE WATER USE CONTROL IN SUDAN
COMMUNITY
SHEIKH
VILLAGE WATER COMMITTEE
TANKER TRUCK OWNER
MECHANIC
CLERK
COMMUNITY DEVELOPMENT AGENCY
NATIONAL WATER CORPORATION
SOURCE: SAME AS IN CHART 3

CHART II

FARM MAP

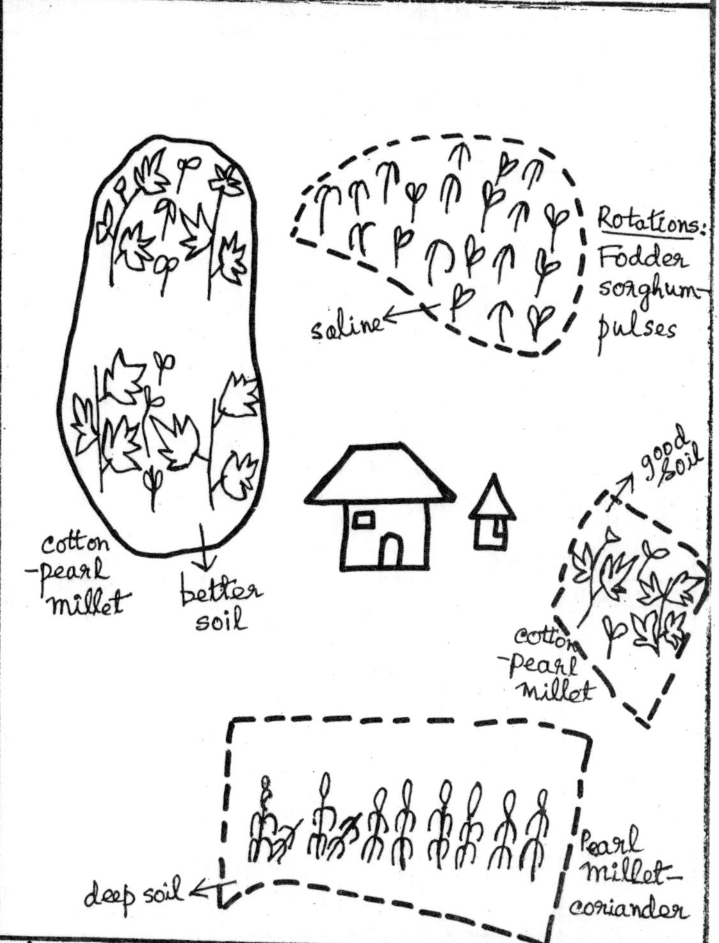

NOTE: FARM PROFILE OF MR. PAI PANDIAN'S FARM, T. MEENAKSHIPURAM.

SOURCE: SAME AS IN TABLE 2.1, CHAPTER-2.

CHART 12

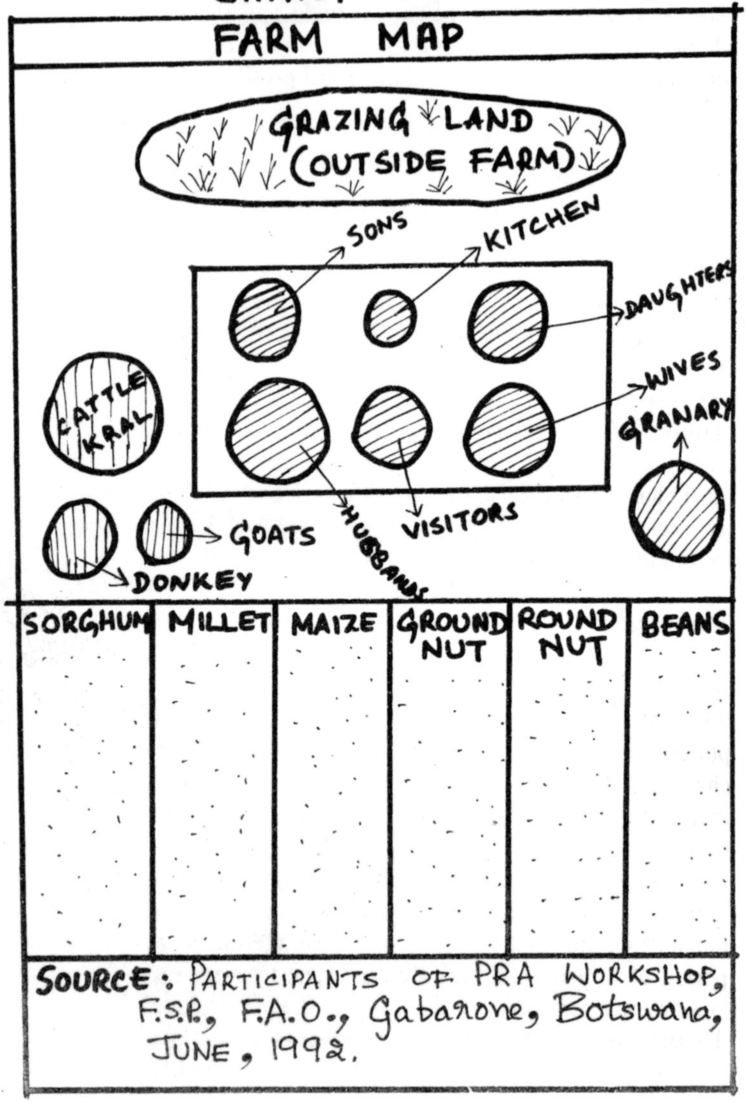
FARM MAP
GRAZING LAND (OUTSIDE FARM)
SONS
KITCHEN
DAUGHTERS
WIVES
GRANARY
CATTLE KRAL
GOATS
DONKEY
HUSBANDS
VISITORS
SORGHUM
MILLET
MAIZE
GROUND NUT
ROUND NUT
BEANS
SOURCE: PARTICIPANTS OF PRA WORKSHOP, F.S.P., F.A.O., Gabarone, Botswana, JUNE, 1992.

(k) Historical Profile

Both past and future profiles of village and villagers are possible through PRA methods. In a historical profile, the villagers provide an historical account of how different aspects of village life have changed over the years. It can then be used for probing various aspects of quality of life of rural people and the different changes which have taken place over a span of years. A historical transect or a time line are different forms of historical profile.

Historical Transect

A historical transect can be done with a group of elderly villagers or with a single elderly person who has knowledge of their village for a long number of years and is able to provide a historical account of the village conditions. It can be done separately with males and females to bring out the difference in perspectives. The historical context can help in knowing the major events and changes in conditions which have taken place in the past for e.g., changes in cropping patterns of resource-poor farmers, changes in kinds and number of trees in the village, traces of environmental degradation, infrastructural changes in the village and others. Chart 13 depicts a historical transect for crops, animals, farm power and yields in an Indian village for the period 1940 to 1991.

Time Line

In the method of time line, elderly villagers narrate their life histories. Since it is often difficult to remember the exact dates of important changes, a villager can be facilitated to broadly connect such changes with major events, political regimes and thus, summarise major events and changes that have taken place during his/her life time.

It was through the method of time line, as shown in Chart 14, that information was given by an elderly villager on the historical wages, quality of food and environmental degradation in a village over a period of 70 years. As indicated in Chart 14, wage rate of a poor villager named Sri Achaiah of village Madhapur (Andhra Pradesh), India went up from Rs. 0.06 paise (Indian currency) per day in 1920 to Rs.15.00 per day in 1990 but the value of money had fallen drastically.

CHART 13

HISTORICAL TRANSECT

	cotton	pearl millet	sorghum	finger millet	green grazing	bullock	tractor	Yield
CROPS, ANIMAL, POWER, YIELD / Year							(HIRE)	
1940	Karun-ganni local	Nattu-Cumbu local	Chenj Cholapn local	Natty Kappai local	Poovani local		–	
1970	Karun-ganni local	local	local	local	local		–	
1979	Lakshmi improved	improved	improved	local	local Anjugam			
1989	LRA 5166	Maha-rastri Wcc 75 local	Co.4 K-tall local	local	local Anjugam			
1991	LRA 5166	Wcc 75 X-10 local	K-tall local	local	local Anjugam			

NOTE: HISTORICAL TRANSECT FOR CROPS, ANIMALS, FARM POWER AND YIELD, VILLAGE: T. MEENAKSHIPURAM, PARTICIPANTS – FARMERS AND ELEPHANT GROUP.

SOURCE: SAME AS IN TABLE 2.1, CHAPTER 2

CHART 14

TIME LINE			
APPROXI-MATE YEAR	WAGE RATE PER DAY	KIND OF FOOD	TREES
1920	Re 0·06	CHAPPATI, GOOD QUALITY RICE	
1940–45	Re 0·15	CHAPPATI, GOOD QUALITY RICE, MEAT OCCASIONALLY	
1980	Rs 1·20	INFERIOR RICE, PULSES, POTATOES	
1985	Rs 10·00	INFERIOR RICE, DILUTED PULSES, POTATOES	
1990	Rs 15·00	RATION RICE, POTATOES, DILUTED* PULSES (*PREPARED WITH MORE WATER, LESS PULSES)	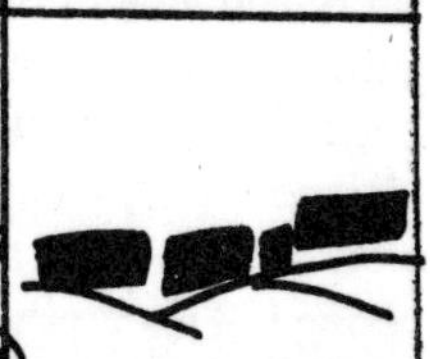

ANALYST – SRI ACHAIAH, VILLAGE MADHAPUR, HYDERABAD, (ANDHRA PRADESH), INDIA.

Hence, even with a considerable rise in wage rate his purchasing power had eroded over the years as a result of which he could purchase lower quantity of food. His quality of food had also deteriorated and he no longer enjoyed the option of having good and nutritious food. On the basis of the time line, he explained his years of hardship which started in the decade of 1980s and continued in 1990s. In these years he did have access to public distribution system to avail of subsidised food prices but he was forced to compromise on the quality of rice and pulses procured from the public distribution system. He was unable to afford meat and also ate less in quantity than earlier periods.

In the time line, he also described ecological degradation of the village over time as witnessed by him. The village and its nearby areas had a rich forest cover with wild life of different kinds which gradually started eroding over the years, and the village at present is full of boulders with almost no trees in sight. One direct impact of the disappearance of forest cover, amongst others, as explained by him was water shortage in the village.

The issue is whether the same information could have been collected through secondary sources. The secondary sources like a questionnaire survey would have provided either an average wage over time, averaged over regions and periods or a range of wages and would have neither indicated any qualitative information nor would have indicated experience of individual well-being and poverty.

(l) Futures Possible

The future scenario can be visualized by rural people through maps, models and diagrams. The future scenario can be envisaged with regard to the outcome of developmental activities in a village, changes in ecology of a village, population changes etc. They can be explained on the basis of maps and models of a village through which the current position and the future possibility can be visualised and explained. This method can be used by rural people to express their expectations of the future shape of their village and the way in which this can happen, the kind of resources which exist and the size of additional resources required.

(m) Time Trends

This method shows quantitative changes over time in different aspects of village life such as yields, population, livestock population, number of trees, area under cultivation, rainfall, time and distance to collect fuelwood and fodder, prices etc. With the help of this method one can directly or indirectly see the increase or decrease of hardship in poor people's lives. A time trend is different from a historical transect or a time line where the former is more precise in giving indication of change (an increase or a decrease) whereas, the latter can show broad movements of different aspects of village life rather than their precise shifts.

Chart 15 illustrates the trend in sorghum price fluctuations in El Obeid, Sudan. It is a way of visualizing changes over time on the basis of data obtained for a selected period (Theis and Grady:1991).

(n) Mobility Map

This shows the pattern of spatial mobility for different sections of a community with respect to different activities. Patterns of group mobility of rural people can emerge from individual maps. Mobility maps of rural people based on socio-economic aspects, gender, age groups and other criteria can indicate the nature of work, wealth, interaction with outside world and interaction within communities and with other communities in a village. It shows the degree of mobility of rural groups and communities and importance of different areas in terms of their different activities. It also indicates location-specific activity profile.

Chart 16 depicts a mobility map of women from Qarara Area in the Gaza Strip. The map shows that the mobility of women takes place on account of different reasons such as work, health, visiting, shopping and education. The most important reason for mobility is work for which women travel from Qarara to at least five places, namely, Gaza city, Noseirat Camp, Derel Belah, Khan Yunis and Rafah. The women travel to Egypt exclusively for the purpose of education. The map also shows inter-linkages between Qarara and Gaza city and Qarara and Khan Yunis whose links are the strongest in terms of mobility of women. The distance, however, between Qarara and Gaza city is far greater than that between Qarara and Khan Yunis.

CHART 15

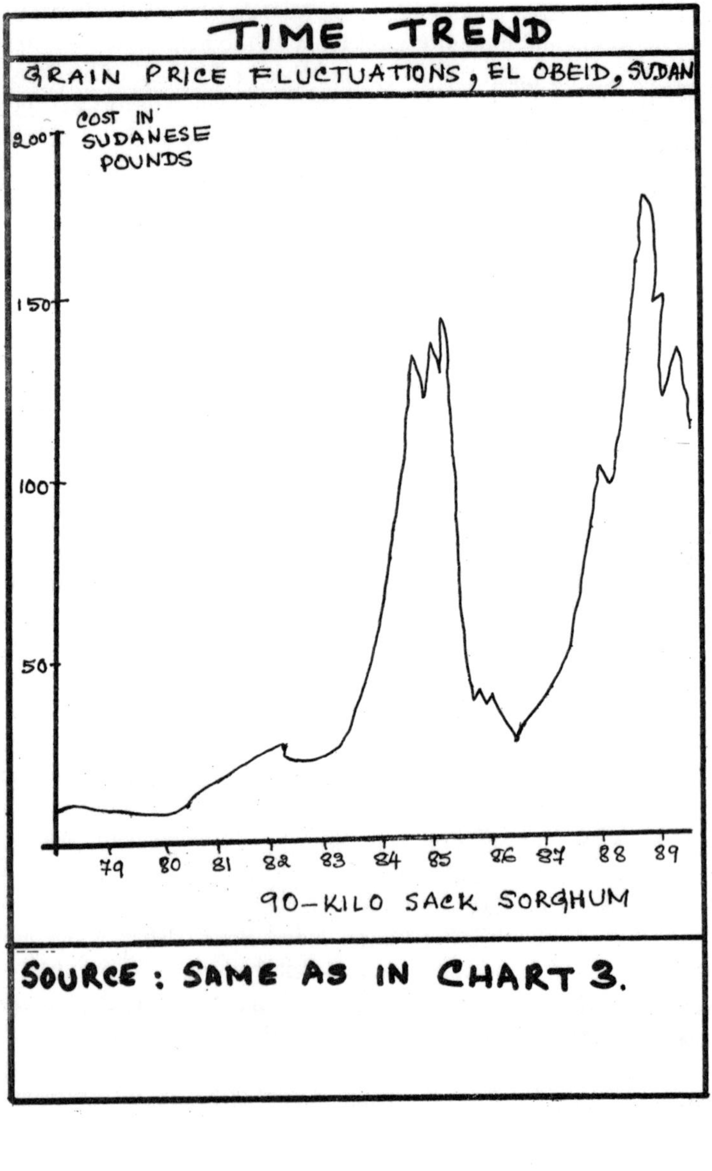
TIME TREND
GRAIN PRICE FLUCTUATIONS, EL OBEID, SUDAN
COST IN SUDANESE POUNDS
200
150
100
50
79
80
81
82
83
84
85
86
87
88
89
90-KILO SACK SORGHUM
SOURCE : SAME AS IN CHART 3.

CHART 16

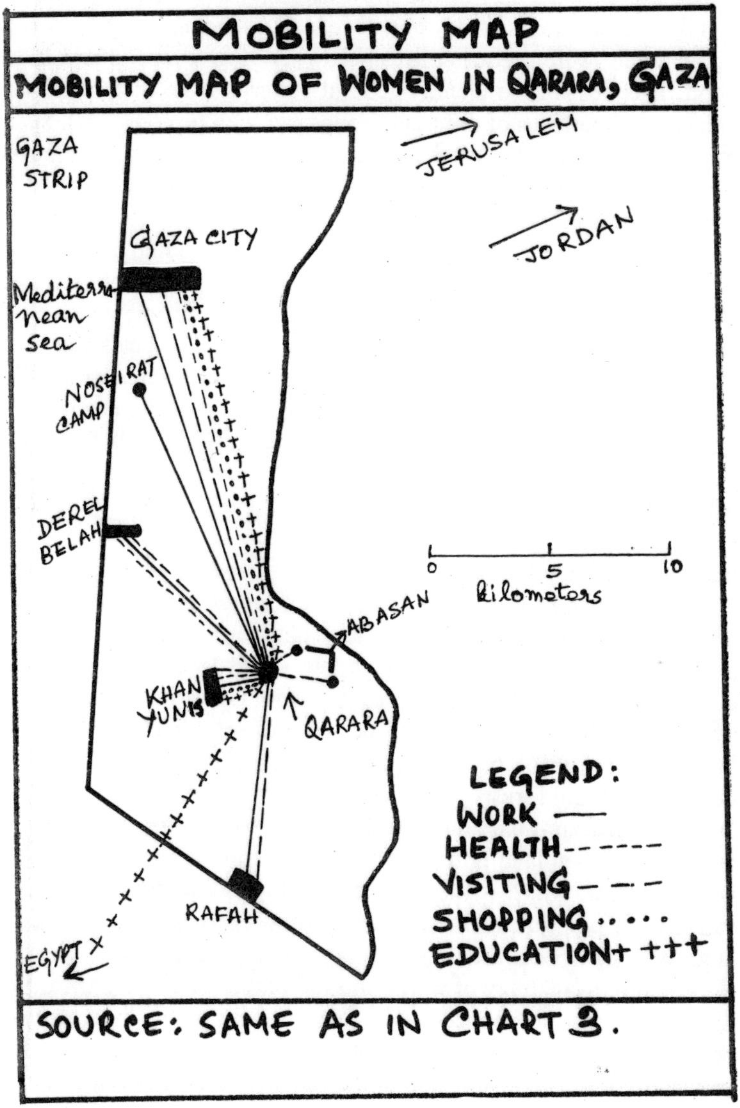
MOBILITY MAP
MOBILITY MAP OF WOMEN IN QARARA, GAZA
GAZA STRIP
JERUSALEM
JORDAN
GAZA CITY
Mediterranean sea
NOSEIRAT CAMP
DER EL BELAH
0 5 10
kilometers
ABASAN
KHAN YUNIS
QARARA
RAFAH
EGYPT
LEGEND:
WORK
HEALTH
VISITING
SHOPPING
EDUCATION
SOURCE: SAME AS IN CHART 3.

(o) Daily Routine Diagram

Daily routine diagrams reflect the kind of activities which one does on a daily basis. It cannot only show the time spent in different activities but also the size of the work involved. For instance, women spend different hours of day in activities like feeding children, cooking, fetching water, grazing livestock, collecting firewood and fuelwood. It is possible to identify general patterns from daily patterns. The general patterns of different groups can then be compared. Such daily routines can also be depicted on a seasonal basis in order to identify constraints and workloads of different groups related to different activities.

In Chart 17, a typical daily routine diagram of women in the Gaza Strip has been presented. The chart shows three groups of activities of rural and urban women namely work at home, income generation and spare time for self as per different hours of a day. The lower part of the chart shows a typical daily activity profile of women where the time spent on various activities at different hours of the day is indicated.

(p) Pie Diagram

Pie diagrams or pie charts indicate parts of a whole in proportional terms. It can show the use of land, water, credit and patterns of income, consumption and expenditure, sources of debt, medicines, kinds of trees etc. in lives of rural people. Chart 18 which shows a pie diagram for land utilisation gives a rough indication of land-use, where agriculture constitutes 45 per cent of total land, followed by hills and river (35%), barren land (10%), school and panchayat (5%), houses (4%) and forests (1%). The chart also indicates the distribution of agricultural land during different seasons, summer, monsoon and winter, when land utilised for agriculture in the monsoon season is 75 per cent, which is the highest as compared to that in summer which is 10 per cent or the lowest. It shows that the proportion of land used for agriculture differs from season to season depending on the climate, availability of water and the nature of crops grown. Pie diagrams show the importance of relative items in the lives of rural people. In this case, the proportion of land used for agriculture also indicates the seasonal hardship of the farmer in terms of livelihood.

CHART 17

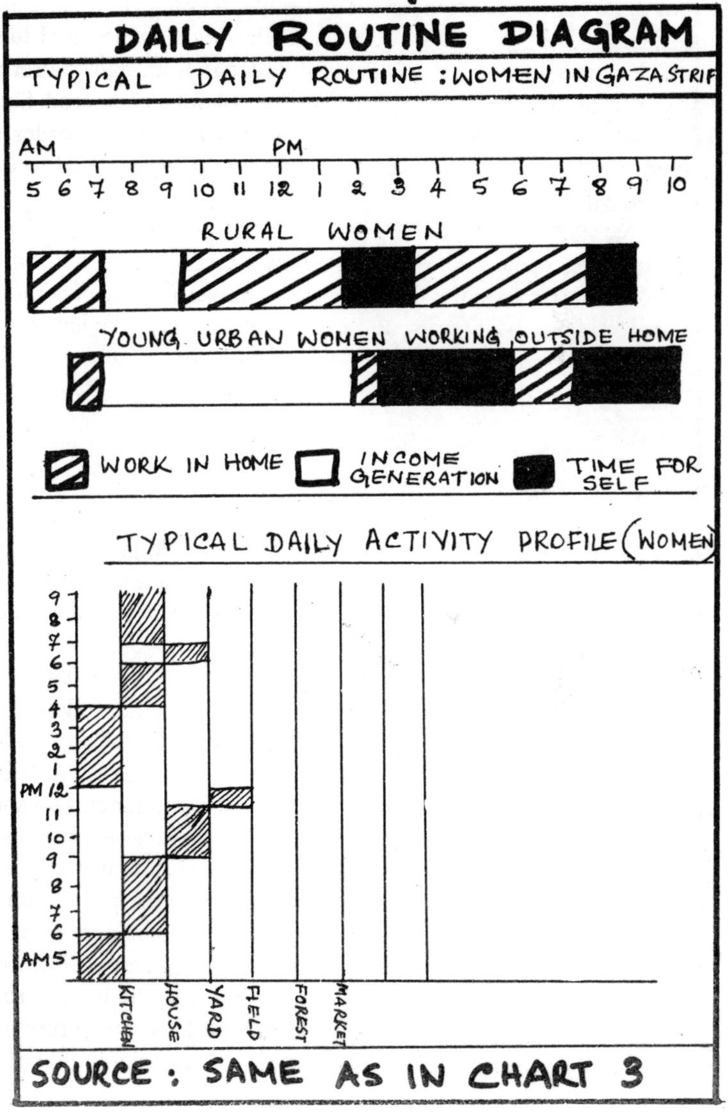

SOURCE : SAME AS IN CHART 3

CHART 18

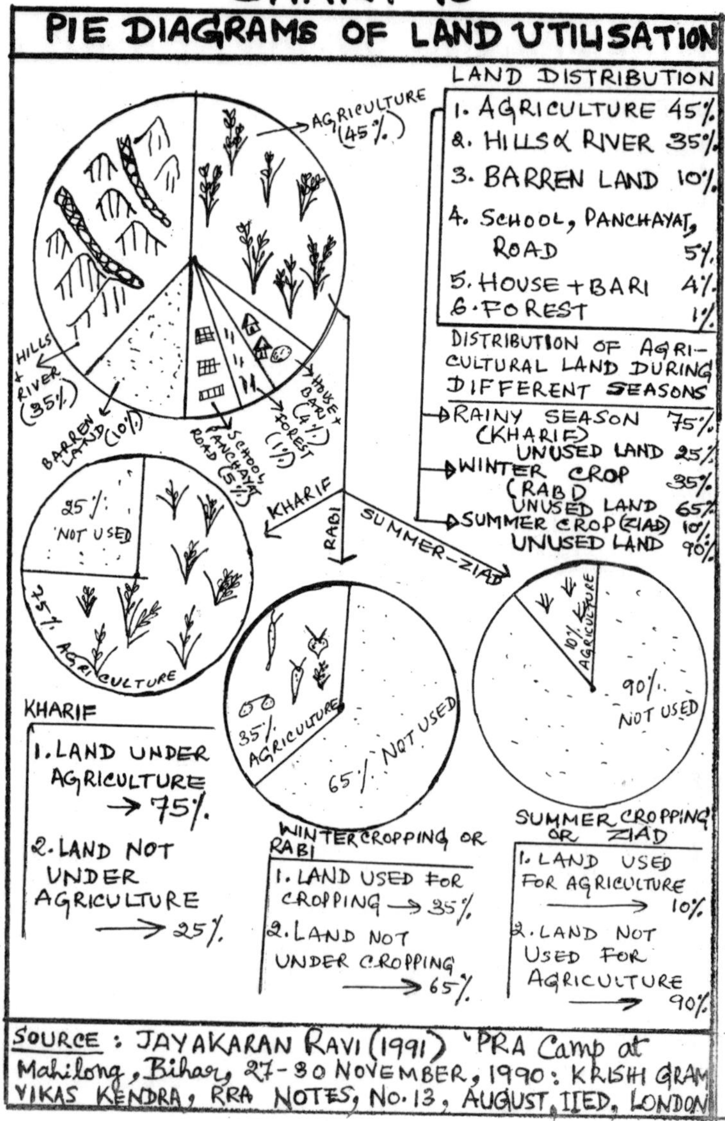
PIE DIAGRAMS OF LAND UTILISATION
LAND DISTRIBUTION
1. AGRICULTURE 45%
2. HILLS & RIVER 35%
3. BARREN LAND 10%
4. SCHOOL, PANCHAYAT, ROAD 5%
5. HOUSE + BARI 4%
6. FOREST 1%
DISTRIBUTION OF AGRICULTURAL LAND DURING DIFFERENT SEASONS
RAINY SEASON (KHARIF) 75%
UNUSED LAND 25%
WINTER CROP (RABI) 35%
UNUSED LAND 65%
SUMMER CROP (ZIAD) 10%
UNUSED LAND 90%
AGRICULTURE (45%)
HILLS + RIVER (35%)
BARREN LAND (10%)
SCHOOL, PANCHAYAT, ROAD (5%)
HOUSE + BARI (4%)
FOREST (1%)
KHARIF
RABI
SUMMER-ZIAD
25% NOT USED
75% AGRICULTURE
35% AGRICULTURE
65% NOT USED
10% AGRICULTURE
90% NOT USED
KHARIF
1. LAND UNDER AGRICULTURE → 75%
2. LAND NOT UNDER AGRICULTURE → 25%
WINTER CROPPING OR RABI
1. LAND USED FOR CROPPING → 35%
2. LAND NOT UNDER CROPPING → 65%
SUMMER CROPPING OR ZIAD
1. LAND USED FOR AGRICULTURE → 10%
2. LAND NOT USED FOR AGRICULTURE → 90%
SOURCE: JAYAKARAN RAVI (1991) 'PRA Camp at Mahilong, Bihar, 27-30 NOVEMBER, 1990: KRISHI GRAM VIKAS KENDRA, RRA NOTES, No. 13, AUGUST, IIED, LONDON

(q) Livelihood Analysis

One application of pie diagram can be for analysing livelihood through the help of pie-charts. This depicts the behaviour and adjustment strategies of households with different socio-economic characteristics. Each household has a strategy or strategies to cope with difficult situations which arise from time to time. Such analysis can account for the size of the household, age and gender composition, wealth, assets, livestock, income and expenditure pattern, debt pattern, consumption pattern, seasonality, income by sources, disease and social obligations.

Chart 19 presents a livelihood source analysis of village Mahilong (Bihar), India with the help of pie-charts (Jayakaran:1991). In 1970, the livelihood analysis was less diversified with 75 per cent of the total number of households dependent on agriculture, while the rest 25 per cent were dependent on the service sector. This scenario underwent considerable change and by 1990 livelihood sources became quite diversified for the households in question. Of total number of households some 80 per cent of the households referred to as group A had a different pattern of livelihood as compared to the rest, i.e., 20 per cent which we can refer to as group B. Of those in group A, around 75 per cent were engaged in the service sector and 20 per cent in paddy cultivation together with 5 per cent in growing of vegetables.

As far as group B was concerned the distribution of sources of livelihood was as follows: Agriculture provided 45 per cent of livelihood, followed by casual labour (40%), vegetable growing (10%), business (3%) and others (2%).

(r) Flow Diagrams

They show the cause-effect relationship amongst different factors and can be effective for understanding the inter-linkages amongst different aspects of rural life. The villagers can be asked to identify different causes of a problem which they are facing and then asked to inter-connect the different aspects so as to have a causal analysis of the problem at hand. They can help in identifying the problems, the determinants, their nature and linkages. This can help in suggesting policies for minimizing constraints and other bottlenecks and can also help in framing of feasible options. For instance, the flow diagram as in Chart 20, is of a village named Krishna Rakshit chak, India which shows how two factors, crop failure and agricultural

CHART 19

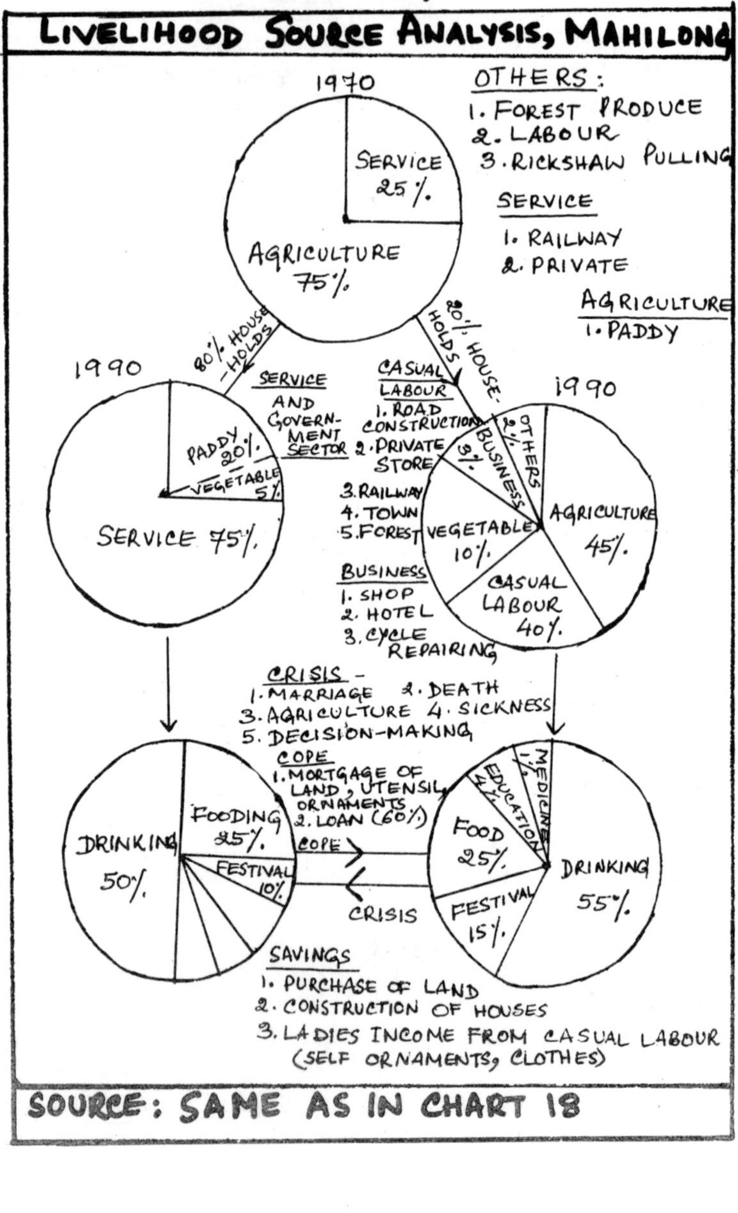
LIVELIHOOD SOURCE ANALYSIS, MAHILONG
1970
SERVICE 25%
AGRICULTURE 75%
OTHERS:
1. FOREST PRODUCE
2. LABOUR
3. RICKSHAW PULLING
SERVICE
1. RAILWAY
2. PRIVATE
AGRICULTURE
1. PADDY
80% HOUSE-HOLDS
20% HOUSE-HOLDS
1990
PADDY 20%
VEGETABLE 5%
SERVICE 75%
SERVICE AND GOVERNMENT SECTOR
CASUAL LABOUR
1. ROAD CONSTRUCTION
2. PRIVATE STORE
3. RAILWAY
4. TOWN
5. FOREST
BUSINESS
1. SHOP
2. HOTEL
3. CYCLE REPAIRING
1990
OTHERS 2%
BUSINESS 3%
VEGETABLE 10%
AGRICULTURE 45%
CASUAL LABOUR 40%
CRISIS -
1. MARRIAGE 2. DEATH
3. AGRICULTURE 4. SICKNESS
5. DECISION-MAKING
COPE
1. MORTGAGE OF LAND, UTENSIL, ORNAMENTS
2. LOAN (60%)
DRINKING 50%
FOODING 25%
FESTIVAL 10%
COPE
CRISIS
FOOD 25%
EDUCATION 4%
MEDICINE 1%
DRINKING 55%
FESTIVAL 15%
SAVINGS
1. PURCHASE OF LAND
2. CONSTRUCTION OF HOUSES
3. LADIES INCOME FROM CASUAL LABOUR (SELF ORNAMENTS, CLOTHES)
SOURCE: SAME AS IN CHART 18

CHART 20

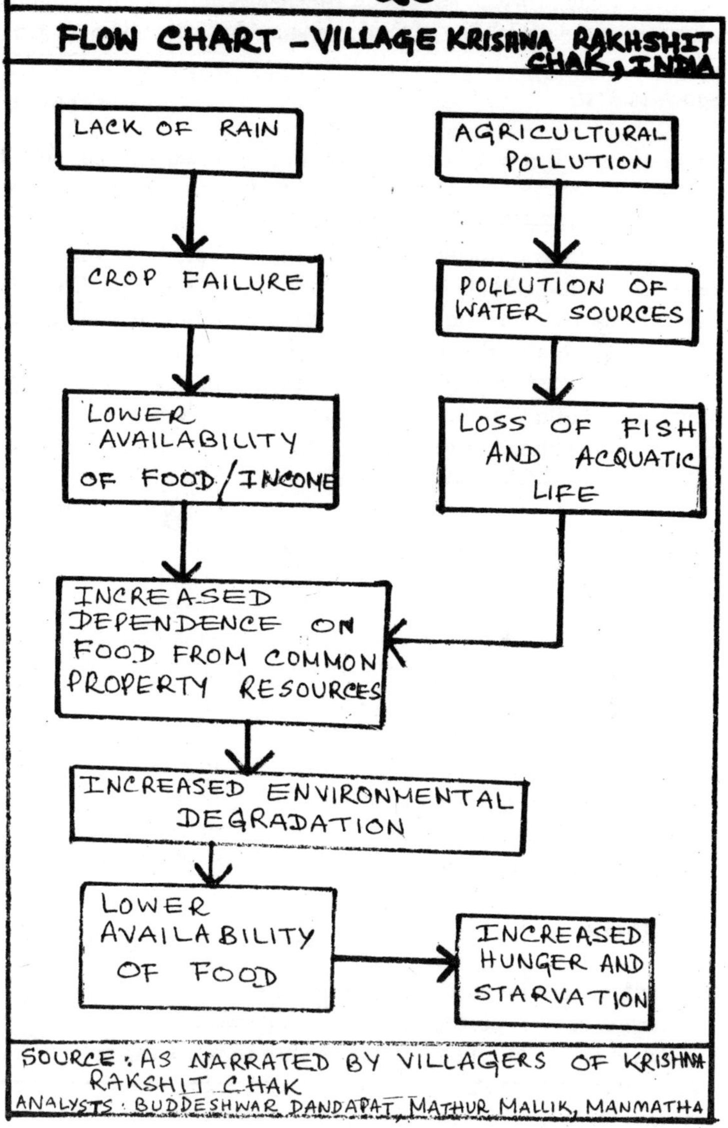
FLOW CHART – VILLAGE KRISHNA RAKHSHIT CHAK, INDIA
LACK OF RAIN
AGRICULTURAL POLLUTION
CROP FAILURE
POLLUTION OF WATER SOURCES
LOWER AVAILABILITY OF FOOD/INCOME
LOSS OF FISH AND ACQUATIC LIFE
INCREASED DEPENDENCE ON FOOD FROM COMMON PROPERTY RESOURCES
INCREASED ENVIRONMENTAL DEGRADATION
LOWER AVAILABILITY OF FOOD
INCREASED HUNGER AND STARVATION
SOURCE: AS NARRATED BY VILLAGERS OF KRISHNA RAKSHIT CHAK
ANALYSTS: BUDDESHWAR DANDAPAT, MATHUR MALLIK, MANMATHA

pollution have led to increased impoverishment and decreased food availability in a resource-poor village. Lack of rain has led to crop failure which has lowered the availability of food/income. This, in turn, has led to increased dependence on common property resources, some of which have been affected by agricultural pollution leading to lower availability of food and increased starvation.

Impact Analysis

Impact analysis is a type of flow diagram. It is an impact diagram of the effects of any activity. The effects can be both favourable and unfavourable on rural livelihoods. The impact diagram shows the impact point and the linkages established (or disrupted) as a result of interventions made (Shah, Bharadwaj and Ambastha: 1991). Chart 21 shows the impact diagram of an irrigation tank in Gadechi village, India, in which the first-tier and second-tier impacts have been shown. The major impact is on the fields from a series of socio-economic and other impacts (second-tier impacts) which have taken place in the livelihood of the farmers, for eg., increase in food consumption, more children joining school, more income etc.

Systems Diagram

A systems diagram depicts a system underlying village life or that of an individual villager and helps in understanding the mechanism and constraints. It is a combination of a farm map with a flow diagram. In Chart 22, systems diagram shows a farm profile and flows of a small farmer in a village in Pakistan. It indicates the relationship between inputs and outputs and flows of output and location of different crops, water bodies and other structures on the farm. The intra-farm flows between each components are also described with the problems involved and the local responses (Guijt and Pretty:1992).

2.3 **Sequencing**

PRA methods can be used in different sequences for appraising different aspect of rural perceptions. Much depends on the objectives at hand, the kind of data required and the use to which the data would be put. There can be different ways of sequencing of methods and using them in different combinations so as to increase their efficiency and utility in the kind of PRA being pursued. The strength of the methods increases with appropriate sequencing and greater information is generated in the process. Different issues can be explored and analysed with methods used in different combinations. A social map and wealth ranking can be followed by a transect walk in those areas of a village where the poor people are concentrated in order to learn about their problems, opportunities and limitations. This can be followed by farm maps and livelihood analysis so as to know more about the crops grown and the soil conditions and the technology used by rural poor and the kinds of livelihood they have.

This can be followed by seasonality diagrams to have information about various related aspects. All these can help in appropriate interventions by State or NGO, through project formulation and planning. The sequence can take a couple of days depending on the convenience of the villagers, the rapport-building and the facilitation skills of outsiders.

In another sequence, a resource map can be followed with a food calendar and a matrix scoring and ranking of wild trees. This can lead to placing of wild trees on the resource map so as to locate them in a village. Such matrix scoring can be useful for planning a tree nursery.

In case of planning and implementing programmes for 'poorest of the poor', the villagers can participate in wealth ranking to identify the groups involved. A social map can be drawn followed by wealth ranking so as to know the poor people, their assets and characteristics. Then individual households of the 'poorest of poor' can be approached for their livelihood analysis and the kind of support they look for in terms of the programme to be implemented. The criteria for evaluation of the programme and its monitoring can emerge from the rural people.

Sequences can be both short and long. The length of the sequences would depend on the topic at hand, the willingness, energy and time of the villagers and the information generated. Some topics can take more time than others and can involve sequencing of several PRA methods to reach the core. However, there can never be any hard and fast rule on sequencing since much depends on the situation at hand, the objectives of a PRA exercise and the way in which it takes shape. This is the novelty of PRA where it differs from situation to situation. It is a creative activity whose form and process are difficult to predict beforehand.

CHART 21

IMPACT DIAGRAM

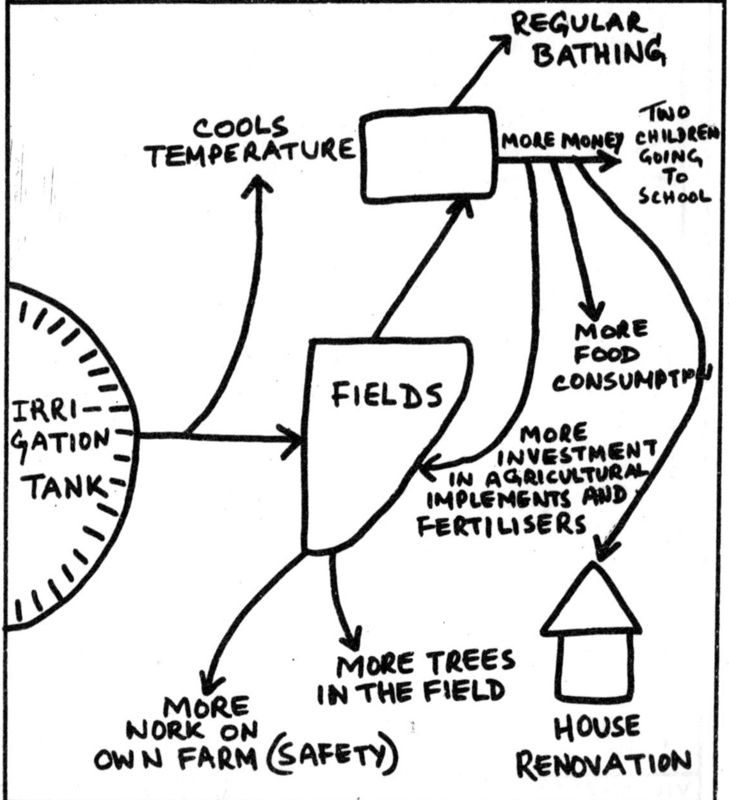

NOTE: IMPACT DIAGRAM OF IRRIGATION TANK IN GADECHI VILLAGE, MADE BY SAVSI BHURA (FARMER) IN SURENDRANAGAR DISTRICT.

SOURCE: SHAH PARMESH, BHARADWAJ GIRISH AND AMBASTHA RANJIT (1991), 'FARMERS AS ANALYSTS AND FACILITATORS IN PARTICIPATORY RURAL APPRAISAL AND PLANNING' IN RRA NOTES, NUMBER 13, AUGUST, IIED, LONDON.

CHART 22

FARM PROFILE AND SYSTEMS DIAGRAM

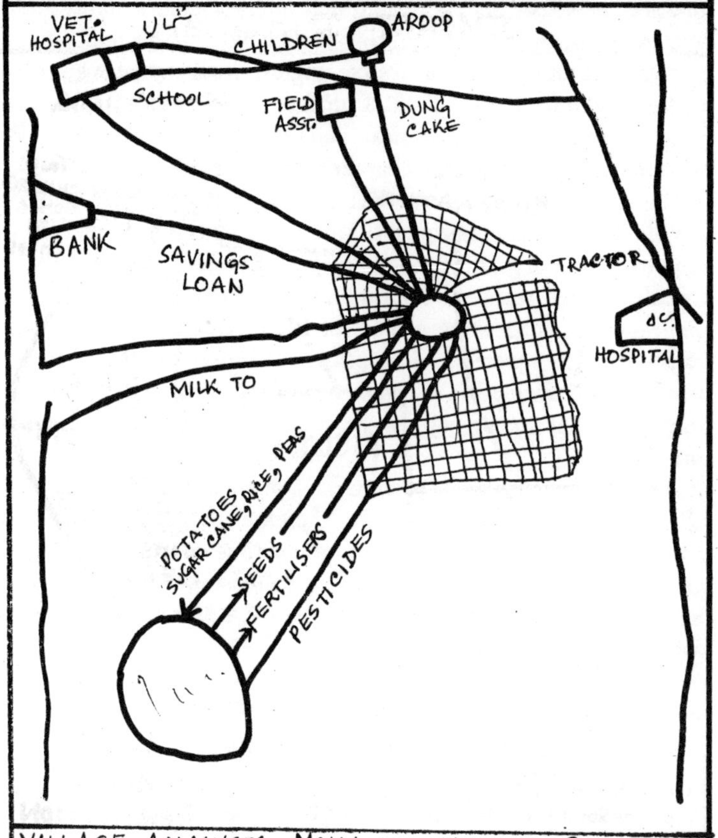

VILLAGE ANALYSTS – MOHAMMED MALIK AND GHULAM QADIR
FACILITATORS: NASRULLAH JAN, M. ASGAR, HUMERA MALIK, MOHD. KHALIQ, 17 FEB, 1992, AROOP.

SOURCE: GUIJT IRENE AND PRETTY JULES N. (ed.) (1992), PARCIPATORY RURAL APPRAISAL FOR FARMER PARCIPATORY RESEARCH IN PUNJAB, PAKISTAN, SUSTAINABLE AGRICULTURE PROGRAMME, I.I.E.D., LONDON, JUNE.

Summary

Chapter 2 is a discussion of the different PRA methods and the indigenous knowledge sources in rural areas. Local histories, stories, folklore, practice, beliefs, traditional management systems and village analysts can provide materials for having a better understanding of rural communities from diverse angles. Such sources can provide background information about a rural community in terms of its culture, socio-economic, political and ecological trends. The PRA methods described in this chapter, include both indirect methods supportive of PRA and those that involve direct participation of rural people. There is a wide range of direct methods, which include participatory mapping and modelling, participatory transect walk, historical transect, seasonal diagramming, ranking, scoring and others. Diagramming is an integral part of PRA. Diagrams enrich discussions, help in revealing perceptions and priorities and in cross-checking of information through group interactions. Each method whether 'visual' or 'verbal' can be used in its own way to approach rural issues.

The chapter also has a section on sequencing of PRA methods in different combinations so as to increase the efficiency of such methods in a PRA exercise. However, there is no fixed format for sequencing. It would vary from session to session. Much depends on the situation at hand, the objectives of a PRA exercise and the way in which it takes shape.

REFERENCES

Burgess, Robert G., (1990), *In the Field, An Introduction to Field Research*, Contemporary Social Research Series, General Editor: Martin Bulmer, Routeledge, London.

Dewees Peter, (1989), 'Aerial Photography and Household Studies in Kenya', *RRA Notes*, Number 7, September, IIED, London.

Grandin Barbara, (1988), *Wealth Ranking in Smallholder Communities: A field manual*, Intermediate Technology Publications, London.

Guijt Irene and Pretty, Jules (1992), *Participatory Rural Appraisal for Farmer Participatory Research in Punjab, Pakistan*, IIED, London.

Jayakaran, Ravi, (1991), 'PRA Camp at Mahilong, Bihar, 27-30, November, 1990: Krishi Gram Vikas Kendra', *RRA Notes*, Number 13, August, IIED, London.

Mascarenhas, Jimmy and Prem Kumar, P.D., (1991), 'Participatory Mapping and Modelling: Users' Notes', *RRA Notes*, Number 12, July, IIED, London.

McCracken, Jennifer A., Pretty, Jules N. and Conway, Gordon R., (1988), *An Introduction to Rapid Rural Appraisal for Agricultural Development*, Sustainable

Agriculture Programme, IIED, London.

McCracken, Jennifer, (1989), 'Diagrams for Participatory RRA', *RRA Notes,* September, IIED, London.

Mearns, Robin, (1988), 'On Oral History and Local Calendars: Experiences in the Field in Papua New Guinea', *RRA Notes*, Number 3, IIED, London.

Mearns, Robin, (1989), 'Aerial Photographs in Rapid Land Resource Appraisal, Papua New Guinea', *RRA Notes*, Number 7, September, IIED, London.

Mukherjee, Neela (1992), 'Villagers' Perceptions of Rural Poverty Through the Mapping method of PRA', *RRA Notes*, Number 15, IIED, London.

Pretty, Jules, (1988), 'Portraits and Stories', *RRA Notes*, Number 3, IIED, London.

RRA Notes, (1991), Number 13, August, IIED, London.

Sandford, Dick, (1989), 'A Note on the Use of Aerial Photographs for Land Use Planning on a Settlement Site in Ethiopia', *RRA Notes,* Number 6, IIED, June.

Scoones, Ian, (1988), 'Learning About Wealth : A Example From Zimbabwe, *RRA Notes*, Number 2, October, IIED, London.

Scoones, Ian, (1992), 'Wealth ranking: Insights into patterns of Rural Differentiation in Southern Zimbabwe', typescript, Sustainable Agriculture Programme, IIED, London.

Shah, Parmesh, Bharadwaj, Girish and Ambastha, Ranjit, (1991), 'Farmers as Analysts and Facilitators in Participatory Rural Appraisal and Planning', *RRA Notes*, Number 13, IIED, London.

Theis, Joachim and Grady Heather M., (1991) *Participatory Rapid Appraisal for Community Development, A Training Manual Based on Experiences in the Middle East and North Africa*, IIED & Save the Children Federation .

3

APPLICATIONS OF PARTICIPATORY RURAL APPRAISAL

Applications of PRA are varied and growing. In this chapter, we describe selected applications of PRA relating to selected themes. The selected areas of application presented below are those of poverty, ecology and well-being, gender and health. It is important to state that any application of PRA is unique in its own way, the process and the methods used being different from situation to situation. Hence, in the applications presented here, one should not look for any fixed patterns, process or methods to be used for any of the themes considered in this chapter. One should rather see them in the light of experience gained in the area of theme-based applications of PRA. Each application adds to our chain of experiences in PRA as a learning process. Such applications tend to bring out the multiple use of PRA to understand and appreciate different dimensions of any topic.

3.1 Poverty and Well-being

The first application is in the context of poverty and well-being in a study of two villages. These relate to wealth grouping as done by rural communities through the PRA method of social mapping. These case studies show essentially two inter-related points (a) grouping of households according to local people's criteria of poverty and well-being; and (b) the criteria for identifying poor households linked with different aspects of village life.

3.1.1 *The Process of Rural Communities' Participation*

The process for seeking community involvement in the villages described below, was to draw the villagers together near a village school or a tea stall or some other common location and explain to them the reason for visiting their village. The reason as stated to the villagers by the PRA team was for purpose of research in order to know more about villagers, their perceptions, their problems and opportunities. Generally the villagers appeared enthusiastic to gather together and meet the team of outsiders. At the beginning, mostly the male residents of the village and the children gathered. After some time, the female residents joined the group and closely observed the other villagers. Eventually, most of them, especially the males were actively participating in the PRA exercise.

These villages are located in the state of West Bengal in India and the socio-cultural setting did make a difference to community participation for the PRA exercise. For example, the female villagers did not feel inhibited from being present in such community participation.

To start with, it was a session of rapport-building with the villagers and the PRA team introducing one and another. Once the introductions took place the villagers were informed about the purpose of visit by the PRA team which was to study their conditions and to learn about their viewpoints. They were asked to describe their village and their day to day living so that the PRA team members could know more about them. Gradually the villagers were requested to draw a social map of the village including the households and land-use patterns and explain it on that basis. The mapping method was used to elicit community responses in identifying the different groups of poor and ranking them accordingly. The entire exercise of mapping and grouping of households was done by the villagers. On average, the villagers took some three to four hours to map the entire village and explain the basis of grouping of households. In case of differences of opinion the villagers were able to sort them out amongst themselves through intense discussions.

The PRA methods of mapping and wealth grouping of village households were used by the villagers to identify the different socio-economic groups of households, rank those groups, identify the 'poorest of the poor' and move upwards to other groups. In this process, the villagers also explained the criteria of such grouping of different households.

First, the villagers mapped their entire village including the households on a paper with a pencil. Then they identified the 'poorest of the poor' households in the village by marking these households on the map. They also described the characteristics and reasons which made these households lie at the bottom line of poverty.

For the purpose of identifying the next group of poor, the question posed to the villagers was: "Which households were slightly better than the 'poorest of the poor' and what were their characteristics?" The villagers identified different groups of poor households than the bottom group along with their specific conditions and characteristics.

The villagers marked each set of households differently with different symbols. They distinguished between different layers of poor households ranking them from bottom and enumerating their characteristics until all households in the village were classified. As and when the different layers of households were identified the group used coloured pens in order to distinguish between different kinds of households and the landuse pattern in the villages under discussion.

3.1.2 *Village Case Studies*

In the month of January 1991, two villages namely Krishna Rakshit Chak and Kalsigeriya in Kharagpur block I, Midnapore district of the State of West Bengal in India were selected with the help of district administration of Midnapore on the basis of their location from headquarters, socio-economic characteristics and number of households. The villages can be described as 'poor' with less than 100 households and remotely situated. The village named Krishna Rakshit Chak is an interior village and has an approach road from a national highway while Kalsigeriya is remotely situated from the district headquarters, interior in location and not easily accessible in absence of proper networking of roads.

Village: Krishna Rakshit Chak: This is a village inhabited by poor tribals. It mainly consists of landless labourers belonging to the 'Lodha' tribe, many of whom own tiny pieces of land, as a result of the land reform measures adopted by the state government of West Bengal. On the basis of the village map (see Chart 23) the villagers ranked the village households by the criterion of annual food availability because food was a scarce commodity for most of the households. This was directly linked to the capacity of near-by forests and ponds to provide sustenance, besides agricultural crops. Households at the bottom of the wealth ranking groups were the ones which had the lowest availability of food on an annual basis.

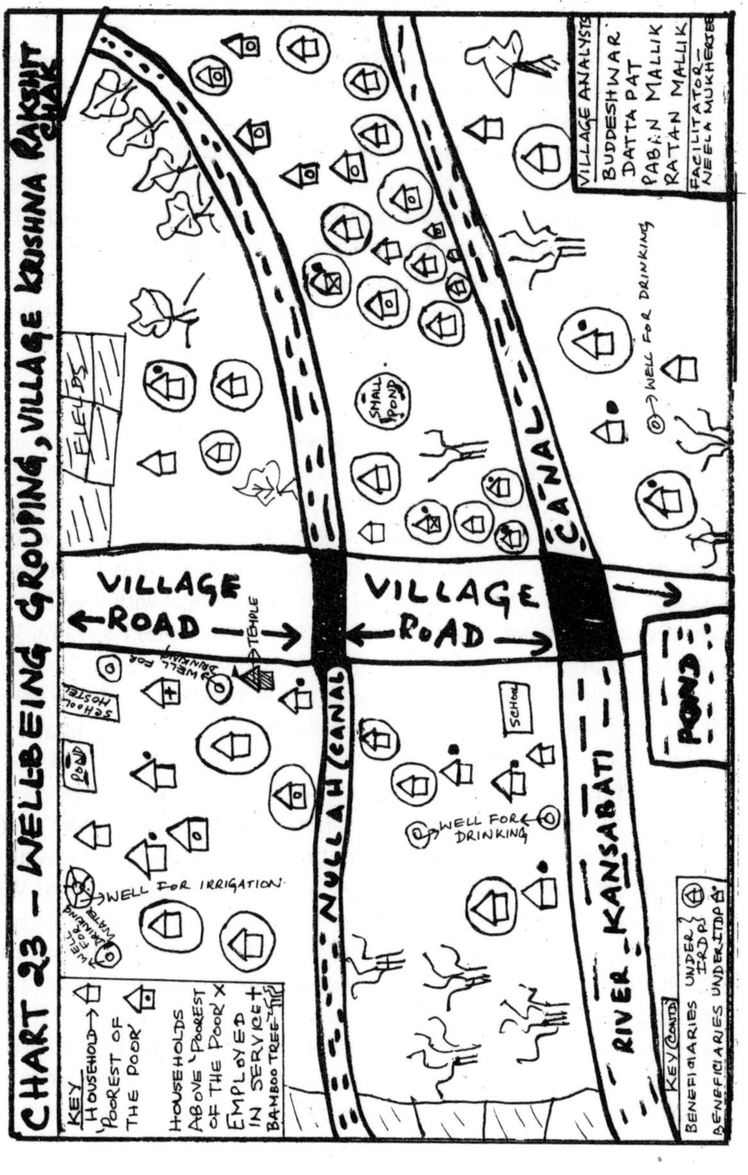
CHART 23 - WELL-BEING GROUPING, VILLAGE KRISHNA RAKSHIT CHAK
KEY
HOUSEHOLD 'POOREST OF THE POOR'
HOUSEHOLDS ABOVE 'POOREST OF THE POOR'
EMPLOYED IN SERVICE
BAMBOO TREE
VILLAGE ROAD
VILLAGE ROAD
TEMPLE
WELL FOR DRINKING
SCHOOL HOSTEL
POND
WELL FOR IRRIGATION
WELL FOR DRINKING
FIELDS
SMALL POND
NULLAH (CANAL)
CANAL
SCHOOL
WELL FOR DRINKING
RIVER KANSABATI
POND
VILLAGE ANALYSTS
BUDDESHWAR
DATTA PAT
PABAN MALLIK
RATAN MALLIK
FACILITATOR - NEELA MUKHERJEE
KEY (CONTD)
BENEFICIARIES UNDER IRDP
BENEFICIARIES UNDER ITDP

The villagers explained their concept of well-being which was described in terms of different linkages with agricultural crops, the forests and ponds, public intervention measures and others. They linked agriculture, common property resources and state interventions in the village, all of which provided alternative modes of subsistence. In any year, food from agriculture lasted a certain number of months, after which most of the villagers generally were dependent on the common property resources in and around the village. Historically, their dependence on common property resources provided them with a high degree of sustenance. However, with rapid degradation of the common property resources and deforestation, their quality of life had deteriorated rapidly. The village ponds from which they generally caught fishes and sold them or consumed them had major problems of pollution. Many of the fishes were diseased due to increased 'water pollution' and had died in large numbers. This problem was a recurring one over the recent years. The forest cover had dwindled, leading to greater vulnerability of those dependent on them. The forest laws also barred them from getting much benefit from the reserve forests. The year 1991, was in particular, a harsh year since the yield of the paddy crop was much lower than earlier years despite good rainfall. According to them this was because of a natural factor described by them as the crop having 'insufficient' sunlight. In selected years there was some seasonal employment offered by the forest department which would contribute in improving their living conditions especially during the lean seasons. Such employment opportunities were no longer available.

The base for food availability was weakened with poor harvests coupled with degradation of ponds and forests and absence of employment opportunities in the forest department. Their well-being had deteriorated in terms of food availability and their access to common property resources and many of them were virtually forced to starve over longer periods.

One factor which had contributed to the psychological well-being of some villagers, in recent years was the ownership of land due to land reforms. These were the same lands which they used to cultivate earlier for their landlords before introduction of land reforms. The land reforms gave them ownership of tiny pieces of land which was mentally satisfying although not economically viable in terms of subsistence. Given the small size of land, they could at best have a small hut to live and grow one or two trees.

Village: Kalsigeriya: Kalsigeriya is a remote village in terms of its distance from district headquarters and also in relation to road networks and is not easily accessible. This village lies in a single cropped area and is affected by floods every year. There are 42 households all belonging to the scheduled caste (a group recognized officially to consist of some selected castes from bottom in the caste hierarchy of the Hindu society in India).

Using household mapping (see Chart 24), the villagers distinguished between three different groups of poor households. The extreme poor group had no land, little food availability during a year, not many working hands and a large number of dependent family members, both young and old who were not capable of productive work. Some from the group were single widows as heads of households. They were all deficit households. They hardly had enough to eat throughout the year and on account of the degradation of common property resources like forests and ponds they were even more food-insecure. Their impoverishment had increased in recent years. They went without proper food on several days per year. The next group of poor households was considered slightly 'better off' and had one or two acres of land. They had some working hands who were able to contribute towards household income and with all their efforts the households were just able to fulfil their consumption requirements.

The remaining groups were comparatively better off and had around four acres of land generally of better quality than others. Some of their household members had jobs outside the village and they were much more comfortable in terms of household income, food availability and purchasing power.

3.1.3 *Indigenous Criteria of Poverty*

The villagers seemed to have a mental checklist which they were referring to for grouping of households. This was the checklist for determining their criteria for well-being. The villagers identified poor households on the basis of the conditions and causes of poverty prevailing in the households. Their checklist looks like the following: one, food availability including wild food, during a year was a significant factor for the villagers in grouping of poor households. Two, the size of landholdings and its productivity was an important consideration for the villagers for identifying higher groups, while noting that land alone was not enough. Its productive capacity was equally important. Three, the number of dependents was another consideration apart from food availability and land holdings.

CHART 24 - WELL-BEING GROUPING, VILLAGE KALSIGERIA
PATHARGHATA KHAL (CANAL)
POND
MORROM ROAD
TEMPLE
POND
POND
MORRUM ROAD
POND
BIG POND
TOWARDS DHANGHORI VILLAGE
KUTCHA ROAD
KUTCHA ROAD
KUTCHA ROAD
KEY
POOREST HOUSEHOLDS OF THE VILLAGE →
BETTER HOUSE HOLDS OF THE VILLAGE
Beneficiaries covered under IRDP →
Beneficiaries covered under MT →
VILLAGE ANALYSTS
RAMAPADA DEY
UTPAL DOLAI
GITA DALAI
BIKRAM CHAND DOLAI
JITEN BHUMIA
JHARESHWAR DOLAI
VILLAGE KALSIGERIA
FACILITATOR-
NEELA MUKHERJEE
23.1.1991

Environmental degradation had accentuated the uncertainty of food availability from common property resources and had increased the incidence of poverty. Common property resources lent support in several ways. For many, such resources formed the basis of their livelihood, for others it supplemented income, food, fuel and other requirements and also provided sustenance during difficult times. Environmental degradation reduced the quality of life for the poor. It led to increased deprivation. The poor were no longer able to fall back on the environment for food, water, work, medicines, fuelwood and clean air especially during lean periods and in years of crop failures. The degradation of ponds, common pastures, river beds, decline in the number of trees and shrubs, in and around the village, decline in area growing them, decline in quality of water and the degradation of forests as sources of food, fodder and fuelwood had directly affected their sources of livelihood, quality of living, its standard and costs and health.

The physical degradation of common property resources has important implications for sustainable development. First, the physical degradation and reduced support of common property resources following their degradation directly increases poverty of rural poor. Second, support provided by common property resources in terms of options to rural poor is that the opportunity cost of using common property resources is much lower than that of market forces or even public intervention measures. Degradation of such resources, decline in productivity and increasing number of people relying on them for sustenance indicate increasing incidence of poverty. This point has also been reiterated in other studies (Jodha:1991). Based on the entitlement approach (Sen:1981, Dreze and Sen:1990) which concentrates on factors determining the bundle of commodities over which an individual or an household can establish command there has been a net fall in endowment (for instance, degradation of common property resources offsets acquisition of land-holdings).

The piece of land received through agrarian reforms by the state was not able to sustain them primarily because of the size and quality of land. However, owning small pieces of land-holdings was mentally satisfying. The indicators used by rural communities under reference for ranking of households are presented in Table 3.1 and their relative comparison is presented in Table 3.2.

TABLE 3.1: Criteria used by Rural Communities of Village Krishna Rakshit Chak and Village Kalsigeriya for Ranking of Households

(i) Food availability
(ii) Landholdings—absence, ownership and size
(iii) Productivity of land-holdings
(iv) State of agricultural crop whether good or bad
(v) Common property resources — its support
(vi) Ownership of assets other than land
(vii) Number of dependents/working hands
(viii) Beneficiaries of state intervention through employment and other programmes
(ix) Jobs outside village

TABLE 3.2: Villagers' Criteria: an Inter-Comparison of Factors of Poverty

Groups	Village Krishna Rakshit Chak	Village Kalsigeriya
Group I- bottom rank of poverty	lowest availability of food especially during lean seasons	no land, no assets, little food availability, not many working hands, high dependency ratio
Group II- Households ranked above group I	better availability of food in terms of months	little land, more working hands, just able to manage food requirements
Group III- Households ranked above group II	better availability of food than that of group II	more land, better quality jobs outside village, enough food availability

Table 3.2 presents an inter-comparison of factors of poverty and well-being and grouping of households in two villages. The villagers use a multitude of criteria from food availability to jobs outside village.

3.1.4 *Other Studies in Wealth Grouping/Ranking*

There are different methods of wealth ranking in use other than that done through social mapping. Such exercises have shown a host of local criteria for wealth grouping/ranking. In a wealth ranking exercise (Sarkar:1991) in Mahilong village in the state of Bihar, India, the villagers used a complex set of criteria for ranking of 142 households into four groups of 'poor', 'so so', 'well' and 'very well'. Some of the criteria used were the capacity of the family to feed from its own produce, ownership of house and well, small family size, owning plough and animal, having consumer durables like television/cycle/ motor cycle, having outside jobs, absence of drinking habits and having police contacts. On most of these criteria, the 'poor' and 'so so' groups were marked by their absence.

In another study (Shah:1990) in a Gujarat village, on the basis of an exercise for classifying economic status of 249 households, community meetings were held with individuals and focus groups who at first classified a selected list of households into four categories of economic well-being on the basis of which the rest of the households were classified. The emerging criteria ranged from health, education, asset ownership, credit worthiness, size of house, land ownership, part-time jobs to the number of dependents. The sequence of classification was based on indicators of economic well-being of which some were its determinants.

3.1.5 *Reflections on Rural Community's Perceptions of Poverty*

Selected issues related to socio-economic classification of poor in a participatory framework require clarification.

Participation of village community implies participation by people belonging to different income groups, castes and creeds. In this context, it has often been experienced that approaching poor people is not an easy job. They tend to remain segregated and generally keep themselves away from outsiders, officials, extension agents and many of them do not attend meetings. Even when they attend meetings they seldom express their opinions. This, however, did not creep in as a problem in conducting PRA in the case studies of Indian villages presented above, since the villages were poor with lesser inequalities amongst the villagers in terms of socio-economic disparities.

However, in many other cases, locating poor people in a village can be a serious problem. There can be ways to overcome such problems. One of such ways adopted in a study in Lushoto district Tanga region in Tanzania is mentioned below (Smith and Sender:1988). In this study, the most effective means of locating poo turned out to be via the primary schools through identifying the ab sentee students from their records. Primary education in Tanzania i compulsory from age seven to age fourteen and there was a seriou problem of absenteeism which was directly related to poverty c those households to which they belonged. Generally, it was seen that absentee school children or their parents were working as agricultural wage labourers.

One important issue is that of absolute vs. relative poverty. People's perceptions of poor households would differ from village to village. Poor people in one village according to its inhabitants may not be considered poor by residents in another village. In some villages, everyone might fall below a certain range of income, and yet they would point to the relatively poor amongst them. In this context, it may be mentioned that the relative indicators for identifying poor households would come from the village community and their grouping or ranking of households would be on that basis. Based on rural perceptions the state can then apply an absolute poverty criterion as a cut-off line for approaching rural poor.

Another issue, often raised is that perceptions of poverty tend to carry implicit cultural judgements which may not be in the best interest of the groups concerned. For e.g., in many rural settings, widow's plight may be ignored altogether when villagers are being asked about socio-economic groups. After all, communities are complex entities and may have differing opinions amongst themselves. Further, groups such as women, ethnic minorities or religious minorities may find it difficult to participate in community gatherings (Borrini:1991).

In this context, it may be suggested that the influence of cultural judgements can be offset to a considerable extent through intercomparison of maps done by different groups. In order to take care of such biases different groups of households based on age, occupation and other criteria can make their own maps and the maps can then be matched to analyse the omissions and errors, if any. For purposes of 'triangulation' or cross-checking visits can be made to the households drawn on the maps to learn more about the validity of the maps made.

With regard to wealth grouping by rural communities it is often pointed out that there are difficulties and inconsistencies in judgements of affluence and poverty which may not necessarily be solved with villagers' own perceptions of poverty. For instance, there can be (i) problems of intra-household distribution of poverty; and (ii) a case in which a villager may choose to live very frugally but may be quite 'well off'. It may be mentioned in this context, that the village system is generally informal and interactive and hence the information flow amongst villagers is considerable. Regarding the problem of intra-household distribution of poverty individual households can be approached and other methods of PRA can be used to study intra-household disparity. Female villagers can also be approached for more information on the same issue since they are the ones who are the victims of discrimination as far as intra-households aspects of poverty are concerned.

It is often remarked that if communities' perceptions of poverty are used to single out recipients in government programmes then it is sure to become prone to manipulation by rural people. This fear is quite unfounded because the formation can be cross-checked and validated in different ways. There exists plenty of room for cross-checking of wealth grouping/ranking done by rural communities and also looking into related grievances and complaints from households. In essence, such issues can be sorted out through greater participation of villagers and not by lesser participation. Cases of manipulation are theoretically possible in a participatory framework but there exists no rational basis for concluding that grouping or ranking of poor in all villages are bound to be manipulated.

It is also argued that as the need for culturally appropriate frameworks is being recognised the tools of the social science researcher should also be culturally appropriate. In this context we describe below another illustration (Grosvenor-Alsop:1989). In a village in North Bihar, India, where caste plays a major role it was expected that a house might be ranked as poor or wealthy according to its relative caste position (low or high). However, the factors common to the respondents' definition of wealth were ownership of livestock, access to land (type, amount and tenure), the number of household members in employment and sources of income. Since not much reliable data were available on the last factor it became difficult to validate it.

3.1.6 *Indigenous Criteria and Conventional Yardstick*

Income or expenditure, as a standard indicator of poverty and well-being has major problems associated with its use. The first question is of using either current income or permanent income or both. Current income can vary from hour to hour, day to day and month to month. Hence measured income of an household in any period is at best a crude average indicator of quality of life not able to reflect the complexity and diversity of rural livelihoods. Members of households are engaged in different activities at different times of the year. This is especially true of the lean seasons. The rural poor work as agricultural labourers, gather, consume and sell things collected from common property resources, hunt, migrate to towns, run services like bullock carts, rear animals and make different items at home to sell. They continuously adjust their strategies for reducing their risks and to maintain their livelihoods which involve a complex range of activities.

Perhaps, gains from all such activities can be expressed in terms of money income but whether this is feasible or not is the question. Apart from feasibility, the other question relates to the complexities of the activities involved and their inter-linkages. Income, as a standard criterion, can distort proper understanding of rural livelihoods and quality of life. At best it can present a partial picture in the maze of multiple sources of subsistence of rural poor where many activities tend to be underperceived especially those of women. Economic valuation of different activities remain a complex issue. Some activities do not fall within the purview of economic livelihood for instance, some can work under conditions of bondage or even beg or borrow.

As reflected above, in the village case studies, some factors determining poverty go much beyond income such as assets, accessibility, social status, environmental degradation, household dependency ratio, land holding and its quality. All of them may be correlates of income, but, income, as a proxy variable, tends to obstruct the proper understanding of processes and linkages of poverty and the complexities arising from interaction of ecological and socio-economic processes. Inclusion of such relevant variables, both quantitative and qualitative, can explain the process of poverty, indicate their influence on rural livelihoods and also help in deriving meaningful policy measures.

As far as household income is concerned there is also a problem of data collection as past experience indicates. The rural questionnaire surveys have gross limitations in reflecting rural realities. A study (Scoones:1992) brings out the limitations of rural surveys in understanding of wealth differences by stratifying households on the basis of indicators of 'wealth' chosen by analyst from outside. The study is an application of the method of wealth ranking in an agro-pastoral community in Mazvihwa communal area, southern Zimbabwe, Africa. It has compared qualitative rankings as done by local people, the survey materials and statistical cluster method. Local rankings include a variety of indicators, both qualitative and quantitative, which reflect important aspects of differentiation, not all of which can be picked up by a survey of assets and income levels. Survey has a restricted time period in the context of past events which can also play an important role. Not only such one-off surveys suffer from non-sampling biases but also the exogenous poverty indicators are inadequate to reflect the complexities of rural settings.

Any indicator which is not representative of the diversity and complexities of poverty can at best be taken as a starting point and improved upon by incorporating field-level realities so as to increase its effectiveness for better understanding of rural realities and redesigning and restructuring programmes for rural upliftment. Hence there lies much scope for improving the method of questionnaire survey. This is illustrated with the following study on poverty (Smith and Sender:1988) in Lushoto district, Tanga region of Tanzania. In the year 1986, a questionnaire was constructed and revised on the basis of the kinds of possessions and types of houses of different income groups. A hundred households were interviewed and the analysis of poverty was undertaken on the basis of a possession score on kinds of houses, whether metal roof or non-mud walls and on selected items including consumer durables like light, watch, radio, bicycle and number of pairs of shoes, beds, mattresses, chairs, coats and other similar items. Presence of these items constituted major improvements in people's well-being. The possession score through survey was used instead of any measure of income as an indicator of socio-economic status. The score was closely correlated with factors such as ownership of land, animals, access to education, contact with extension agent etc.(Smith and Sender:1988).

Income as a standard indicator of poverty, which is a money income indicator, is rigid and deficient and is not able to incorporate or reflect significant aspects of poor households which constitute the major determinants of the quality of life of rural poor. If rural people are given a chance to do wealth-grouping of their village and identify the poor households from the bottom, the selection of the intended beneficiaries would be much more realistic than the efforts undertaken by outsiders going from house to house to prepare household surveys of income and expenditure of rural households.

Summary

The above section presents two case studies of wealth ranking by rural communities in two villages named Krishna Rakshit Chak and Kalsigeriya, both in Midnapore district of the state of West Bengal in India. The rural communities of the two villages grouped different households in the village on the basis of their criteria which they perceived as important in terms of poverty and well-being. The indigenous criteria which emerged from the PRA sessions in the two villages were in terms of land ownership, accessibility to common property resources, food availability, state of agricultural crops and others. The section also discusses selected issues about people's perceptions and PRA methods and a comparison of income as a conventional yardstick for wealth ranking *vis-a-vis* rural people's criteria.

3.2 Understanding Rural Women Through Participation

The present section seeks to illustrate gender aspects of rural life based on learning from field experiences. It focuses on rural women and brings out different aspects of the topic through case studies in selected villages. The methodology applied is that of PRA and the case studies relate to gender analysis and reflect on aspects such as the nature of perceptions of rural women *vis-a-vis* rural men, their expertise and role in selected activities, their nature of work and daily routine, their deprivation through food discrimination and their ranking of problems and prioritisation. Each sub-section of this section is based on a different case study to focus on aspects described above.

3.2.1 *Gender Perceptions*

In this section, the main theme of analysis is differences in perceptions of rural women *vis-a-vis* rural men which can make for differences in understanding and appreciation of rural issues. The importance of perceptions of rural women can hardly be overemphasized. Their role in society, their problems, priorities and capabilities, if truly appreciated can lay the foundations of a gender-based approach to rural development much stronger and productive than that of earlier decades when gender-based issues were not of any consequence. The rural woman as a mother, as a partner in a rural household and as a member of rural society and the nation at large performs functions which are both critical and burdensome, many of which are not always visible and tangible in terms of economic output. Strengthening the position of rural woman through complementary inputs would mean strengthening of her capabilities and performance which would get reflected in her contributions to village life, in particular, and to the progress of the nation in general.

3.2.1a *Difference in Perceptions by Gender*: Why should rural women have perceptions different from rural men? Some of the reasons can be as follows. Their up-bringing, values, beliefs and customs can make them see things in a different perspective than those of men. Their nature of work and their experience can also influence their perceptions considerably than those of rural men. Their role in society is different and hence, their problems and priorities are also different from men. Their decision-making capacity through direct participation can help in identification of their problems, their preferences and ways and means to resolve them.

3.2.1b *Gender Perceptions Revealed*: Aspects of gender can be revealed through participation of both females and males in rural areas. Participation, voluntary in nature, would relate to villagers expressing their views and opinions, their knowledge and beliefs, their priorities and preferences and their problems and ways of resolving them whether by themselves or in collaboration with others. Communication with villagers based on trust and friendship can help in making them participate in a free and relaxed manner.

In rural areas, participation of men is relatively easier than that of women. Rural women may show reluctance to participate for many reasons. They are often busy in their households and other places of work and may not be able to find enough time for participation. Some of them may feel inhibited to participate for reasons such as lack of confidence, family pressures, customs etc., while others may take time to gather courage to express themselves. On many occasions, their voices are dominated by those of males and they feel less confident to present their views. On account of the reasons mentioned above participation of rural women may not be easily forthcoming. We may feel tempted to leave them out and not to approach them because of the difficulties involved in interacting with rural women. This, at best, would be professionally convenient but of little use in eliciting rural perceptions by gender.

It is important that a facilitator interested in participation of villagers is able to establish rapport with both female and male villagers so as to generate their interest in participation. A team of facilitators with both men and women in it would be better than one which consists of only male members. For effective participation, both verbal and visual methods are important. Verbal interviewing of men and women in separate groups or together can be through a series of questions of which some are prepared beforehand while others are framed according to the situation at hand. The visual participatory methods of mapping, ranking and seasonality or other methods can also be used by separate groups of men and women or as one group where both the groups actively participate together. Visual methods can reveal gender perceptions and preferences, quantitative and qualitative measurements, judgements and comparisons of issues at hand which are otherwise hidden and obscure.

3.2.1c *How Gender Perceptions Differ ?*: A case study is described below to show how gender perceptions differ. The case study relates to hamlet Zhadghar of village Zhadghar, a tribal village in Thane district of Maharashtra. The hamlet consists of 48 households, most of which belong to groups of small and marginal farmers and landless labourers.

The villagers formed into two groups of 12 to 15 each – one group of women and the other group of men. These two groups were asked to prepare village maps depicting different households, roads, water bodies and other structures. Without losing much time, the group of men started drawing the map on the ground with coloured chalks, while the women group was not so quick. To start with, the group was slightly hesitant but after some time it got over the inertia and started drawing the village map on the ground.

After about ninety minutes, there were two maps of hamlet Zhadghar ready on the ground, one by men and the other by women. The maps depicted households, other structures, sources of water, roads etc. The maps were broadly similar yet dis-similar in some respects. One major point of difference was the omission of footpaths (except one) in men's map which had village roads drawn on them in greater detail. One reason to explain the difference was to do with the relevance of roads and footpaths to men and women. The womens' map had the footpaths shown quite prominently. The footpaths were being daily used by the village women for collection of fuelwood, fodder and water.

The women were the ones who collected fuelwood and fodder from nearby forests and water from wells located near the village. In the map done by the village women, the footpaths stood out clearly and boldly more in terms of relevance than proportion. The men were aware of these footpaths but did not find them of much relevance as found by women. They were more interested in the roads that they generally used for going to different areas outside the village in search of work.

Another interesting aspect of gender perceptions came to light with wealth-grouping done by the two groups. On completion of the village maps by the men and the women groups (see Chart 25 and Chart 26) both groups were asked to point out those households which they considered as 'worst off' in the hamlet in terms of their socio-economic position. The response of the two groups were strikingly different. The women group indicated two widowed households as 'worst off' of which one widow was blind in one eye while the other widow's livelihood was dependent on rearing and selling of goats. Both households according to the women group were the most deprived.

On the other hand, the men group identified two male-headed households on the village map which were according to them the 'worst off' in their village. One such household had 5 adults and 3 children and owned no land. While, the adults of the other household were unemployed most of the time and did not have knowledge of the traditional craft of the village which was basket-making.

On probing further into socio-economic grouping done by the two groups of men and women, their differences in perceptions of well-being became clear. For the men group, ownership of land and employment opportunities were important indicators of well-being. On asking the men group about the well-being grouping done by the women it was of the opinion that both the widowed households considered as 'worst off' by the women group owned some land. The widow, blind in one eye, had a small piece of agricultural land which she had lent to some person for cultivation. While the other widow also owned some forest land which she had earlier encroached. Hence, according to the group of men, the two widowed households were better placed than those households which the group thought were 'worst off'.

For the group of women, deprived social status and physical handicap were more important considerations for well-being than ownership of land and employment opportunities. On this basis they had marked the 'worst off' households. The village women did perceive that socio-economic deprivation of the two widowed households accentuated on account of their widowhood and handicapped life. It also showed how social considerations were more important for the women group. Whereas, the group of men seemed to be more practical and perceived economic factors such as land ownership and employment opportunities to be more important than social ones.

CHART 25 - SOCIAL MAP BY MEN

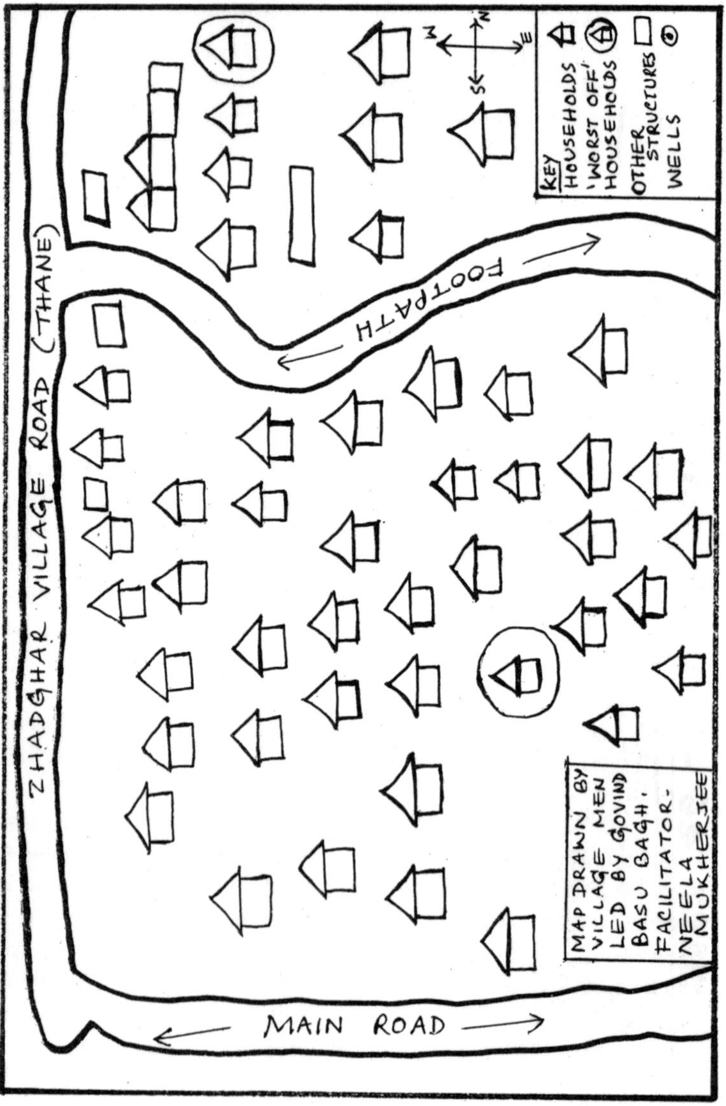

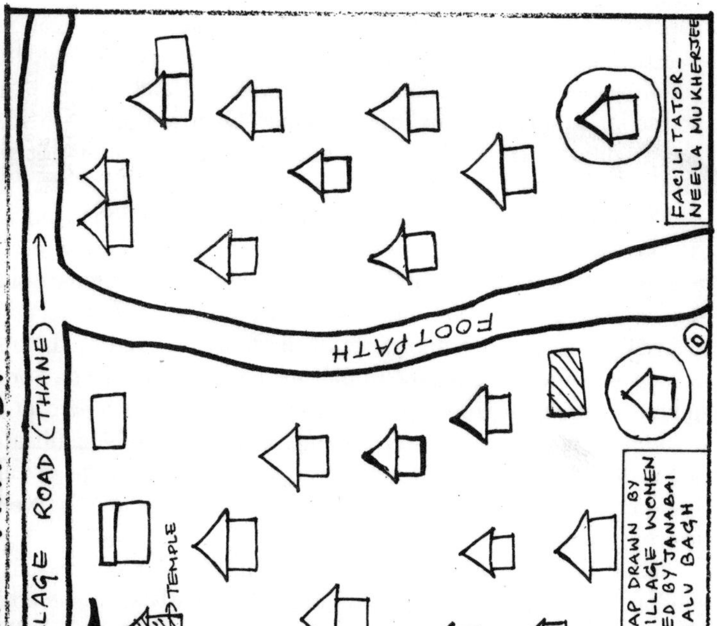
CHART 26 - SOCIAL MAP BY WOMEN
ZHADGHAR VILLAGE ROAD (THANE)
FOOTPATH
FOOTPATH
FOOTPATH
TEMPLE
MAP DRAWN BY VILLAGE WOMEN LED BY JANABAI MALU BAGH
FACILITATOR– NEELA MUKHERJEE
KEY
HOUSEHOLDS
'WORST OFF' HOUSEHOLDS
OTHER STRUCTURES
WELLS
N
S
E
W

3.2.1d *The Participatory Methods and Gender Perceptions*: The above case study brings out gender differences in perceptions of the same village and the relative importance of factors considered for comparisons of well-being. Both verbal and visual methods of participation were used to elicit perceptions from women and men groups. Verbal method of semi-structured interviewing helped initially towards rapport-building with the villagers and to solicit their interaction in a relaxed and open manner. Questions about their village, traditional craft, daily routine etc. helped to generate their interest in participation.

Visual methods of making maps helped the discussion to move on the basis of the village profiles prepared by the men and women groups on the ground. Both the maps helped in comparison of gender perspectives. Without making of the two maps, perceptions regarding the relative importance of the footpaths and roads to the women and the men groups would not have got reflected. For instance, through a semi-structured interview much of such perceptions would have remained hidden. The maps also facilitated identification of households for comparison of well-being. The two groups revealed their perceptions/biases not only through interviews but also through drawing of maps.

3.2.1e *Some Implications for Planning*: Perceptions based on gender need not match. They can differ enormously as shown above. Projects designed for men based on men's perceptions is well taken. However, projects designed for women based on men's perceptions can be ill-designed and inefficient. Further, projects designed for the village community as a whole based exclusively on men's perceptions is incomplete and not fully informed since the perceptions of their female counterparts are not included. For development workers at the grassroot level, it may not be unusual to watch that differences arising out of gender is significant enough to make or mar the appropriateness of development programmes. The gender perceptions can be revealed through participation of clienteles of development, both men and women. It is time that the conventional model of development is challenged and overthrown in favour of gender-based local variants through active participation of rural women and men so as to take care of differences in gender perceptions and to adopt a realistic approach to rural issues.

3.2.2 *Rural Women's Knowledge*

The rural women perform activities which are mostly different from that of rural men. Such activities range from child rearing to household activities and farm operations. Many of such activities are not directly visible and tangible in terms of economic gains. However, the rural women play a crucial role in most rural activities and their participation can be solicited to learn about their knowledge gained in the process of performing such activities. Performing the activities again and again make them well defined and routinised. The activities are integral to rural life and, the women, by tradition, have assumed responsibility for such activities. Such activities are both difficult and time consuming and provide a critical support to rural life.

In order to learn more about any activity in the village one should identify the group/groups which performs/perform it. Direct description of any activity from the performer gives greater details and insights than learning about it from a non-performer. For instance, in order to learn about an activity such as collection of fuelwood which is primarily a woman's job in the village one needs to approach a rural woman rather than a rural man. The rural woman as a performer is in a position to give details of what fuelwood she collects, the frequency and the time spent for collection, the problems associated with such collection etc.

3.2.2a *Seasonal Food Variations*: In this section, a food calendar made by rural women has been described in order to highlight three aspects of village life. One is the knowledge of rural women in the procurement of food, two, their role in such procurement and three, is the seasonality of food availability, its shortage and the dependence of the villagers on wild food.

This is a case study of a village named Krishna Rakshit Chak in Midnapore district of West Bengal, India. The villagers belong to the 'Lodha' tribe and are mostly landless labourers. They had gathered near their primary school building to participate in a discussion about the village life. While discussing about food availability a group of male villagers were requested to show a seasonal food calender to depict the seasonal variations in food and the pattern of their food consumption during a one-year period.

The group of men did not appear very enthusiastic while the women were sitting quietly in a corner and watching them from a distance. To make things simpler the men were asked to show the different varieties of food that they were consuming in that month i.e.

'Magh' or mid-January to mid-February. Some of them tried to give an account of what food they had on that day but were unable to move further than that for quite some time. This made some other men prompt a few food items but again it appeared that the food calendar was not making much progress. After some time, it was quite obvious that the men were not finding enough interest in the food calendar. They appeared more interested in making a village map and discussing about their village rather than discussing about their seasonal food variations. When the group of men became busy in making the village map the women group who were quietly watching them from a distance were requested to make a food calendar in order to show their seasonal food variations.

The group of women showed their interest in making the calendar and sat together to prepare it. They started discussions amongst themselves so as to prepare the calendar. They started preparing the calendar on the ground with 12 stones to represent 12 months. Then, with the help of both stones and pebbles they showed their main items of consumption like rice, potato and pulses where the number of stones indicated the quantum of food. Later they used different kinds of leaves, sticks and twigs of trees to show their supplementary items of consumption such as vegetables, wild leaves, fruits, meat of wild animals, fish, snails, wild water plants etc. However, weights of the supplementary items were not indicated, availability of which varied from day to day even within a month.

3.2.2b *Seasonal Food Calendar*: The food calendar as shown in Chart 27 has some important features in terms of food availability. Eating of rice reaches a peak in 'Magh' (mid-January to mid-February) after which it declines until 'Chaitra' (mid-March to mid-April), to remain stationary until 'Aswin' (mid-September to mid-October), following which it further declines by almost half of the earlier period.

Eating of potatoes follows approximately the same trend as rice for the months of 'Magh' and 'Phalgun' and then declines sharply during the period from 'Chaitra' (mid-March to mid-April) to 'Agrahyan' (mid-November to mid-December) and picks up again in 'Poush' (mid-December to mid-January).

Intake of pulses as a food item is very low in the month of 'Baisakh' and is higher in the months of 'Srabon', 'Agrahyan' and 'Poush' as shown in Chart 27.

CHART 27

SEASONAL FOOD CALENDAR

MONTH \ ITEMS	RICE (NO. OF STONES)	POTATO	PULSES	VEGETABLES	FRUITS	FOOD FROM OTHER SOURCES	OTHERS FROM WILD
MAGH (mid-Jan. to mid-Feb.)	15	13	3	CABBAGE			WILD BORUMS WILD RABBITS
PHALGUN (mid-Feb. to mid-March)	9	11	2	SPINACH			'NEEM' LEAVES
CHAITRA (mid-March to mid-April)	4	4	2	PUMPKIN		FISH AND WILD WATER PLANTS	
BAISAKH (mid-April to mid-May)	4	3	1	'PUI' LEAVES (HERBS)	MANGO* JACK-FRUIT*	FISH, SNAILS AND WILD WATER PLANT	
JYAISTHA (mid-May to mid-June)	4	4	2	'LOTA' LEAVES (HERBS)	MANGO* JACK-FRUIT*	FISH AND WILD WATER PLANTS	
ASHAR (mid-June to mid-July)	4	3	3	'JHINGE'			
SRABON (mid-July to mid-August)	4	4	5	PAPAYA			
BHADRA (mid-August to mid-Sept.)	4	3	3	GREEN BANANA		FISH AND SNAILS	
ASWIN (mid-Sept. to mid-Oct.)	4	3	2				
KARTICK (mid-Oct. to mid-Nov.)	2	4	3	RADDISH LEAVES			
AGRHAYAN (mid-Nov. to mid-Dec.)	2	4	5	TOMATO			
POUSH (mid-Dec. to mid-Jan.)	2	9	6	BRINJAL			WILD RABBITS

NOTE : THE NUMBER SPECIFIED UNDER RICE, POTATO AND PULSES REPRESENT THE NO. OF STONES SHOWN BY VILLAGERS. * SHOW FRUITS OF TREES GROWING NEAR-BY.

WOMEN VILLAGE ANALYSTS – NAMITA MALLIK, BINAPANI DANDAPAT, PRATIMA [illegible] A MALLIK.

DATE : 4.2.19[illegible]

[illegible]IT CHAK, MIDNAPORE

The villagers also have different kinds of seasonal items of food depending on their availability. The deficit in the main items of consumption is filled with supplementary items fetched from the 'wild' and the ponds and sometimes even from the market. Availability of them from the market depends on their purchasing power which is quite low. Most of such sources can hardly compensate for the fall in availability of rice. Hence there is a sharp fall in food intake especially around the months of 'Chaitra' to 'Aswin' which is aggravated during 'Kartik' and 'Agrahyan' as per the food calendar. The women's group pointed out that with erosion of the 'wild' and degradation of ponds, the support received from them as sources of food had declined considerably over time.

3.2.2c *Some Observations on the Food Calendar*: Some of the observations based on the above exercise and the discussions which followed are as follows:

(a) Rural women, in general, are more knowledgeable than rural men in depicting the variety of food which they generally go and collect from different sources.
(b) The variety of food available and the different sources of food are kept track of generally by the village women whether it is from ponds, river beds, forests, wild trees in the village and near-by areas. It is they who are the main performers in terms of collection of raw food, meeting food deficits in households (whether by eating less or supplementing from other sources) and cooking food as well.
(c) The village women try to hedge against low food availability. They tend to switch sources depending on the seasons. It is apparent as shown in the food calendar, that in some seasons more food is available in both quantity and variety such as in the month of 'Magh' as compared to the month of 'Aswin' when not much is available.

3.2.2d *Some Implications for Participatory Planning*: The villagers of Krishna Rakshit Chak are poor and are not in a position to buy enough food requirements. The alternate sources of food from the 'wild' and ponds do provide some support towards food availability. However, as it appears from the food calendar there are limits to availability of wild food in the lean seasons (when they are most needed) and the villagers are forced to go without adequate food and remain hungry. In years of crop failure the situation is further aggravated.

Participatory sessions with women villagers can be conducted to identify women-managed projects on wild trees and plants so as to increase food availability and decrease their hardship and uncertainty in collection of food. Practical suggestions can be sought from the village women for planting of wild plants and trees and their maintenance. The women can be empowered to collaborate in such projects in terms of their time and skills. Projects like way-side agro-forestry can also be taken up by rural women and can be managed by them. Such agro-forestry projects can include seasonal plants whose flower, fruits, leaves, vegetables, roots and stems can be used to supplement the food intake of the villagers. The village women can suggest the plants which they would like to grow. The time spent by rural women in collection of food can be gainfully utilised by them in looking after such projects and sharing the returns from such projects as and when available.

3.2.3 *Understanding Rural Women : Their Daily Routine*

Rural women are generally busy throughout the day mostly in their households. A large number of them also work outside on their own or share outside work with the male members of their households besides having exclusive responsibility of running households. Much of such work is of a routine nature and is repetitive. Rural women generally have a busy schedule to cope up with day to day responsibility. As a result, they seldom find much time for themselves either to relax or to do something different. In a PRA session in village Banstaol, district Tangail, Bangladesh, a group of women were approached in order to learn about their daily routine of activities. They narrated their daily work schedule as described below.

At first, it was a session of rapport building with the women in the village of Banstaol. Later the PRA team enquired about the role of women in farm activities. On this aspect, the women replied that they were actively involved in growing of brinjals and bananas as well as other food crops. Preliminary activities in paddy fields were also done by them. However, they did not practice cultivation. They were basically engaged in supplementary activities in the fields. They explained their work relating to both households and outside their households and listed their schedule of different activities which they perform.

The following is an account of the work done by women in the field as shown in Table 3.3.

TABLE 3.3: Field Activities of Rural Women

(a) Women weed the field once ploughing is over;
(b) For orchards growing banana, the women arrange the soil to heap them together near the roots of banana trees;
(c) It is the women who carry water in earthen pots to water the fields atleast 10 to 20 times a day as required;
(d) They carry food, water and 'hukka' pipe to the field for their household male members;
(e) They carry fertilisers of different varieties to the field;
(f) They pick the grass growing in the field and decompose it for making fertilisers;
(g) In orchards growing bananas they prepare the soil, plant the seedlings, water them and pick weeds.

Apart from work in orchards, vegetable gardens and rice fields the rural women also have a busy schedule of household work. The following is an account of the household work performed by them on a daily basis as shown in Table 3.4.

TABLE 3.4: Daily Routine of Household Activities of Rural Women

(a) Early morning waking up and reciting prayers;
(b) Sweeping the front portion of the hut;
(c) Taking the cattle out from its shed and giving it fodder;
(d) Taking out goats and tying them in places where they can eat on their own;
(e) Sweeping the back portion of the hut;
(f) Cleaning utensils;
(g) Cleaning the children and their teeth;
(h) fetching water for cooking;
(i) Preparing food for household members and serving them;
(j) Getting the children ready and sending them to school;
(k) Fetching water for bathing;
(l) Cooking for lunch and serving;
(m) Giving fodder to cattle and goats;
(n) Tying them at places where they can find more food;
(o) Sweeping and cleaning the house;
(q) Fetching water for cooking;
(r) Cooking food for the evening and serving;
(s) Reciting prayers before sleeping in the night and going to bed.

After completion of household work or during spare time, if any, the rural women generally have other activities to perform. Some of these were described by the group of rural women at the village mentioned above. They are shown in Table 3.5.

TABLE 3.5: Other Activities by Rural Women

(a) To weave mats from local grasses and sell them;
(b) To weave fences from the bamboo sticks cut by them and to sell them;
(c) At the time of ripening of fruits like 'bel', mango, jackfruit, tamarind, borums and 'jalpai', the women help in collecting them while the men pluck them from trees.

The village analysts of the daily activity schedule mentioned above were women named Kadarjan, Mayjan, Kamla Khatun, Sonacham, Hasina and Baleka of Shaplakuree Mahila Samiti of village Banstaol, Mirzapur, Tangail district of Bangladesh.

3.2.4 *Gender Discrimination – Deprivation of Rural Women*

Gender discrimination is practised widely against women in most countries of the world. It begins even before birth, at birth it is reinforced and runs unto death. Such discrimination can be practised in every sphere of life. Many aspects of such discrimination are open while others are hidden and not readily visible. It can be as much in rural areas as in urban areas. The focus of this section is on discrimination against rural women. There can be various aspects of gender discrimination in rural areas such as discrimination in food, work, schooling, job opportunities etc. Many aspects of discrimination are not always visible. However, such discrimination leads to deprivation of rural women.

3.2.4a *Food Discrimination Against Rural Women*: One aspect of gender discrimination is often found in food intake inside households. In matters of food-intake, such discrimination can be of a high order. The answer to who discriminates is a mixed one. Food discrimination can be practised by men by eating 'more' and 'better' than women, or by women where the woman as a mother discriminates between male-child and girl-child, as a mother-in-law discriminates against her daughter-in-law and as a wife eat less than her husband.

One important issue in this regard is that to what extent it exists in rural areas, what are its dimensions and is there a way to understand the nature and extent of such discrimination. One way would be to directly observe and assess such discrimination. The other way would be to learn about the discrimination through participation of those groups of villagers against whom the discrimination takes place, for instance, the rural women.

3.2.4b *Some Effects of Food Discrimination*: Food discrimination as practised in households is not an ideal situation. It tends to have unfavourable consequences for instance, it affects the health of the girl child, health of a pregnant woman, a lactating mother and the women at work. It can also have unfavourable effects on women such as giving birth to a deformed child, proneness to diseases, starvation, anaemia, malnutrition, weakness etc. Apart from physical problems it can lead to psychological deprivation as well.

3.2.4c *Why Food Discrimination is Practised ?*: Food discrimination can be practised for different reasons. Some of the factors explaining food discrimination are as follows:

(a) On many occasions, food discrimination is on account of poverty leading to low food availability in a household. If there is less to eat in a household it is usually the female members who bear the brunt of it.

(b) There prevails a cultural perception that a girl child is inferior to a male child and a woman is inferior to a man and hence the woman and the girl child tend to have food less in quantity and inferior in kind, in relative terms. Based on the above, the eating habits are nurtured from childhood and food discrimination continues.

(c) The discrimination can relate to food and also in the case of special food items such as meat, milk, fish etc. because they are relatively expensive or not easily available.

(d) It can be caused by the spirit of sacrifice of women to eat less and make the male members eat relatively more. In this way both food and money are saved by a household and its daily problem of procuring food is also sorted out.

(d) Another factor is that by nature and constitution some men require more food as compared to women.

3.2.4d *Seasonal Food Calendar and Food Discrimination*: The following account gives an idea of food discrimination practised in village Banstaol of Tangail district in Bangladesh. Seasonal calendars showing comparative quantum of food taken by an adult male and an adult female and that of a girl child and a male child were prepared by a group of women villagers of village Banstaol. The calendars are shown in Chart 28 and Chart 29.

CHART-28 - FOOD DISCRIMINATION

SEASONAL FOOD CALENDAR- MALE ADULT / FEMALE ADULT

MONTHS / ITEMS	CHAITRA		BAISHAK		JYAISTHA		ASHAR		SRABON		BHADRA		ASWIN		KARTIK		AGRAHYAN		POUSH		MAGH		PHALGUN	
	M	F	M	F	M	F	M	F	M	F	M	F	M	F	M	F	M	F	M	F	M	F	M	F
RICE	2	2	6	5	7	6	9	8	9	8	7	6	6	5	5	4	8	7	6	3	6	5	6	5
CHAPPATI	5	4	0	0	0	0	0	0	0	0	0	0	0	0	2	2	0	0	0	0	3	2	3	2
VEGETABLES	1	1	2	2	6	6	10	10	7	7	5	5	4	3	6	4	3	3	3	2	2	2	2	2
PULSES	10	10	5	5	4	4	2	2	3	2	6	6	7	7	7	6	7	6	9	7	8	8	9	9
FISH	1	1	5	2	4	3	2	3	5	2	3	3	8	3	8	2	5	2	4	2	1	2	2	2
EGG	3	2	4	2	3	2	3	2	4	1	4	2	8	3	10	4	9	9	10	9	8	7	7	6
MILK	11	10	5	5	4	4	3	3	3	2	3	3	4	3	2	2	2	2	2	2	2	2	8	8
MANGO	-	-	-	-	4	4	-	-	-	-	-	-	-	-	-	-	-	-	-	-	-	-	-	-
JACK-FRUIT	-	-	-	-	9	6	8	5	-	-	-	-	-	-	-	-	-							

VILLAGE ANALYSTS - REHANA PARVIN AND FERDUSI BEGUM, VILLAGE BANSTAOL, DISTRICT TANGAIL, BANGLADESH

NOTE : THE FIGURES SHOW THE NO. OF SEEDS USED IN SCORING; M STANDS FOR MALE, F FOR FEMALE

CHART 29 – FOOD DISCRIMINATION

SEASONAL FOOD CALENDAR – GIRL CHILD/MALECHILD – ONE YEAR OLD																								
MONTHS / ITEMS	CHAITRA		BAISAKH		JAISTHA		ASHAR		SRABON		BHADRA		ASWIN		KARTIK		AGRAHYAN		POUSH		MAGH		PHALGUN	
	M	F	M	F	M	F	M	F	M	F	M	F	M	F	M	F	M	F	M	F	M	F	M	F
RICE	2	1	3	2	5	3	6	4	6	5	7	6	8	7	6	5	7	6	8	7	9	8	6	5
PULSES	7	6	6	5	4	3	6	4	5	4	7	6	7	6	6	5	6	5	6	5	5	4	7	6
VEGE-TABLES	3	2	4	3	3	2	4	4	4	3	6	5	7	6	5	3	4	3	7	6	6	5	5	4
FISH	2	1	2	1	2	1	3	2	3	2	4	3	5	4	4	3	4	3	5	4	6	5	4	3
EGG	6	4	4	3	3	2	3	2	4	3	5	4	6	5	4	3	7	5	8	7	4	3	10	9
MILK	9	7	4	3	5	3	4	3	4	3	5	4	6	5	6	5	6	3	8	7	6	5	7	6
BANANA	7	3	6	4	4	3	3	2	4	3	5	4	7	6	6	5	4	4	6	5	5	4	8	7
ORANGE	4	3	4	2	3	2	2	1	3	2	2	1	4	3	4	3	4	4	5	4				
MANGO							3	2																
JACK-FRUIT							4	3																
PINE-APPLE											2	1	1		3	2	4	3	5	4				
APPLE													2	1	4	3	4	3			5	4		
PAPAYA											4	3											6	5
BISCUIT	3	1	2	1	2	1	3	2	3	2	2	1	5	4	5	4	5	4	6	5	4	3	7	6

NOTE: SAME AS IN CHART 28; VILLAGE ANALYSTS – SAME AS IN CHART 28

The two seasonal food calendars, one of which describe seasonal food variations of a male adult and a female adult and the other of a male child and a girl child bring out aspect of food discrimination in practice. The calendars give an idea of what kind of discrimination is practised and how it varies from season to season. Such discrimination is present in almost all items of food and increases with tastier and better quality food. The food calendar for adult in chart 28 describes food taken by a male and a female on 8 items – rice, *chappati*, vegetables, pulses, eggs, fish, milk and fruits. The calendar was done on the ground using different kinds of seeds representing different food items. The making of the calendar was followed by an interview in which the women explained that for certain items like rice, vegetables and pulses, the seeds represented weights while for others, like eggs, fish, milk and fruits, the seeds showed frequencies of consumption of those items. The calendar relates to all the twelve months. It shows the seasonal availability and intake of food and the extent of food discrimination.

Chart 29 describes a seasonal food calendar for one year old girl child and male child. The children are given food in turns. The number of seeds depict both weight and frequencies as indicated in the food calendar for adults. The food taken by children increase as their age increases from one year to two years yet the girl child gets relatively less than the male child and the discrimination continues in the long run.

3.2.5 *Understanding Rural Women : Problems and Prioritisation*

Rural women face different problems either on a regular basis or at different times, many of which are not easy to resolve on account of societal perceptions and other factors. The problems can be of different kinds and they reveal them if they find opportunities for doing so. Given a chance, the rural women can describe their problems and prioritise them according to their perceptions. The following illustration gives an account of the problems of rural women in village Banstaol of Tangail district in Bangladesh.

3.2.5a *Prioritisation of Problems by Rural Women*: A group of rural women in village Banstaol prioritised their problems using different number of seeds. The scoring of problems brought to light different priorities of problems specified. They listed 15 problems and scored them on the basis of relative importance perceived by them. Table 3.6 lists the problems and their scoring.

TABLE 3.6: Problems of Rural Women and their Prioritisation

Problems	Scoring by Number of Seeds
(1) Giving of Dowry	20
(2) Husbands desert Wives and Remarry	10
(3) Cruelty and Repression	16
(4) Problem of Drinking Water	12
(5) Shortage of Housing	16
(6) Problem of Medical Treatment	12
(7) Wife-beating	18
(8) Divorce by Husband	12
(9) Large Number of Children	17
(10) Cruelty of In-laws	12
(11) Shortage of Land	15
(12) Problem of Latrine	10
(13) Shortage of Cash	15
(14) Harassment by Fundamentalists	14
(15) Problem of Transport	15

From the scoring above, it appears that giving of dowry is the most serious problem followed by wife-beating and having large number of children. The first problem directly reflects their socio-economic position as regards dowry which they find very difficult to provide while getting their daughters married. Wife-beating causes both physical and mental repression while bearing of a large number of children is a problem which they are unable to cope up with.

The problems mentioned above can be separately grouped into four categories for comparison. These are shown in Table 3.7.

3.2.5b *Some Observations on Women's Problems*: Many of the problems of rural women relate to social problems within households. These are their priority-problems and most of them relate to inter-personal relationships arising from inequitable power structure within households. There are a couple of problems relating to infrastructure, some of which directly affect the work-load of woman and indirectly the physical and psychological well-being of herself and her family.

Shortage of cash is a manifestation of low income and poverty and problem of land is a factor causing poverty. To top it all, the harassment by fundamentalists which is in the nature of a religious problem is also of much consequence to the women who perceive it as a form of repression.

TABLE 3.7: Classification of Problems by Rural Women

Problems	Scoring by Number of Seeds
I. *Social Problems within Households*	
(1) Giving of Dowry	20
(2) Husbands Desert Wives and Remarry	10
(3) Cruelty and Repression	16
(7) Wife-Beating	18
(8) Divorce by Husband	12
(9) Large number of Children	17
(10) Cruelty of In-laws	12
II. *Problems relating to Infrastructure*	
(4) Problem of Drinking water	12
(5) Shortage of Housing	16
(6) Problem of Medical Treatment	12
(12) Problem of Latrine	10
(15) Problem of Transport	15
III. *Economic Problems*	
(11) Shortage of Land	15
(13) Shortage of Cash	15
IV. Religious Problem	
(14) Harassment by Fundamentalists	14

The social problems within households and those relating to fundamentalists arise because the women feel repressed and are not in a position to assert their rights and privileges. It calls for economic and social empowerment of women whether on the basis of actions taken by state or other non-government development organisations. Formation of pressure groups of men and women in village communities or village-level organisations can also play a significant role in diminishing the intensity of the stated problems. The other economic problems of finding cash and owning land are related to poverty and can be resolved through appropriate packages of poverty-reduction programmes.

Summary

In this section, we have discussed selected aspects of gender issues in order to understand and appreciate rural women, their role in society and their basis of perceptions. We saw from a case study that their perceptions tend to differ from those of rural men whether it is perceiving their own village or perceiving of social well-being. We also saw through a case study that the rural women have their own stock of rural knowledge because of the nature of work they perform. Another case study showed that besides their day to day household work for which they are indispensable, the rural women also share responsibilities for farm activities along with men. Their busy schedule does not spare them much time and with whatever time they find they engage themselves in other income generating activities.

Rural women are deprived and discriminated upon in several ways. One such way is that of food intake and the seasonal food calendars of adult male and adult female and that of a girl child and male child, in this section show the food discrimination practised against adult female and girl child. The last section of this chapter illustrates the kind of problems faced by rural women and the way they prioritise them.

3.3 PRA in Health

In this section, we give an account of participation in rural health and selected applications in health PRA. The state of health in many rural areas is in a deplorable condition. Even with health interventions by the state and other development organizations the results from such interventions are not very encouraging. Although numerous primary health centres/clinics have been set up in rural areas our experience at the field level, give enough indications that the resources spent on improving health facilities in rural areas not only appear to be inadequate but on many occasions mis-directed and mis-matched. Apart from a tendency for a mismatch between the supply of facilities and those demanded, the efficiency of the rural health delivery system is also not of a very high order. Neither are the medicines stocked adequately nor are the equipments modernised or the health workers properly motivated. Hence, it is of utmost importance that in the area of rural health, efforts are necessary to put scarce resources to their best use.

This, strongly suggests towards participatory rural health where, on one hand, health workers can have a first hand learning of rural health conditions from the villagers and provide better services, while, on the other hand, the villagers can explain their health problems and demand proper health services. The way would be to directly interact with the villagers and learn of their health requirements and their perceptions in health-related areas. This would give practical idea of how relevant and effective are the health interventions and what more is desirable.

3.3.1 *What is a Health PRA ?*

A health PRA is an application of the methodology of PRA to learn from rural people about issues related to health. It can be done as a part of a general PRA exercise or can be conducted to have a special focus on health.

There is a general tendency amongst us to think that the villagers cannot make us learn about rural health because they are ignorant and mostly uneducated. This is surely a fallacious thinking on the following account. Since the rural people are the victims of poor health conditions in villages it is they who can tell us about their experiences and perceptions. For instance, a primary health centre can be set up by the state to cater to rural health. However, to what extent the centre would succeed in its mission would depend on its acceptability and use by the local people. If the local people do not perceive the need for a health centre for reasons such as availability of indigenous treatment or otherwise in their locality, it may still be important for the health centre to know how it can complement and supplement such treatment which villagers prefer.

In this context, the villagers can participate to make us learn about their health conditions, their kind and nature of illness, the causes, the nature of treatment adopted and their preferences and priorities. Even when formal health facilities exists in a rural area it is desirable to find out how such facilities can be improved and extended and also how the local people perceive the relevance of such facilities.

A PRA in rural health can range from a mere description of certain kinds of illness the villagers experience from time to time, to a participative session generating a rich analysis of conditions, problems, causes, priorities and preferences in the area of rural health. The scope for participation of villagers in rural health is almost limitless, they being the clienteles of our rural health programmes. Hence, health PRA can be of immense significance in poor countries with inadequate health facilities in rural areas.

3.3.2 *Utility of Health PRA*

Both village communities and health workers can benefit from health PRA. This can bring to surface health status of village communities. On that basis, the health workers can learn from villagers about their health status, their priorities and preferences in getting treatment, the medicines they use and the level of health awareness. With regard to occurrence of specific diseases in a locality, the local people would be able to relate its periodicity and frequency. This can give broad indications of the time of health interventions whether from state or other development organizations. Based on such aspects, any agency can impart health education and better treatment specific to location, gender, need, age and other factors so as to improve the conditions of health prevailing in rural areas. The following features can be generated through a health PRA depending on its coverage.

(i) The health status of a rural community
(ii) Frequency of illness and villagers' perceptions
(iii) Sources of treatment of illness
(iv) Local treatment and indigenous medicines available
(v) Number of villagers going without treatment
(vi) Planning health interventions with periodicity as required
(vii) Support for poor villagers for whom health is a critical factor for their day to day living.

For family planning programmes the extent of village coverage can be appreciated through a health map of households. At a glance, it can show which households have adopted family planning, its kind and why others have not adopted it as yet. The participation of those villagers not adopting family planning would throw light on their views on the same subject and their problems in adoption, if any.

3.3.3 *Approaching Villagers*

The issue is how to approach villagers for learning more about rural health. The approach would differ from village to village, from group to group and from individual to individual depending on many factors. Some of these factors are the willingness of the villagers to participate, their seriousness in getting treatment, the symptoms, state of illness, age, gender, periodicity of illness etc.

The following description of a semi-structured interview session in a village in Thane district of Maharashtra, India, provides some interesting insights into probing about the health status of the villagers. A PRA team asked the villagers to describe the kind of illness they suffered from. Their answer was that were not victims of any illness. On repeating the same question in different ways, almost similar answers were received and the progress made in the direction of a health PRA was minimal. However, in a separate session with a female health worker of that village, it was found that most of the women in that village had anaemia. The female worker also expressed that attempts made by her in educating them about their health problems were not of much consequence.

Later in the PRA session, the same villagers were asked about the sources of treatment that they generally adopted once they fell ill. On this, they mentioned about the local 'bhagats' or 'quacks' whom they usually approached for treatment. On asking about the medical facilities available from near-by primary health centre the villagers were of the opinion that the centre was quite far from their village and getting to that centre for a sick person was a major problem not only in terms of transport but also in terms of the expenditure and time involved. Hence, it happened to be their last priority. The PRA team was also interested in speaking to the local 'bhagats' but for some reason they were not available in the village for any discussion.

In a PRA session in another village in Thane district of Maharashtra, India, the villagers appeared quite enthusiastic and came up with their list of health problems. They spoke about vomiting and diarrhoea being their special problems during the rainy season. Such a discussion followed a social map done by the same villagers. The above two illustrations show how a health PRA can be different in different cases. A health PRA can be initiated in many other ways (TISS:1991 & 1992). It can be different both in terms of process and methods in different situations.

3.3.4 *Selected Aspects of Health PRA*

There are various aspects of health PRA. One important thing is to learn about the state of health in a village. Are there any diseases which are rampant in a village or frequently occurring and having unfavourable impacts? These can then be identified by the villagers to have priority considerations, if necessary. A village map can indicate status of health of each household. Such a participatory social map can have the number of members in a household and the state of health of each member. This is best known through mapping of households in a village either in a single map or mapping in parts in case of a village, quite large in size. Participatory mapping can also be done by villagers focussing on different localities in the village. One can have numbers for each household in case names are not possible or one can have identification of households by their names. The map can be cross-checked by visiting each household in the map concerned.

A health map of a village would give broad indications of the health status of the village apart from indicating individual cases. It can show the major illness affecting the village, if any, the age-groups afflicted by such illness, the frequencies of such illness and other details. Such maps can show a broad range of variables relating to health at a particular point of time. They can form a basis for discussions on different aspects such as historical background of certain health problems, the number affected from a certain illness, recovery from that illness etc. They can also form a basis for discussion of the nature of present illness, the symptoms, the treatment, villagers' perceptions of illness and other related issues.

To give some illustrations of the applications of PRA methods in the area of health, it is possible to use seasonality diagrams of diseases to indicate their periodicity and their intensity. Such diagrams can be extended for diseases affecting livestock. The method of matrix scoring can be used to score on health problems and sources of treatment preferred. Other methods like body mapping can also be used for rural perceptions about human body and its working (RRA Notes:1992).

A health map projected with map on wealth/socio-economic grouping/ranking would show the relationship between the two aspects of well-being. It would answer such questions as whether there is a strong relationship between poverty and poor health. Are there any special diseases affecting the poor group ? For example, we shall see in the case study given below, that health map of a village when projected on its social map with wealth grouping show how ill health and poverty in many households go together.

3.3.5 *A Health PRA in a Village*

This is a case study in health PRA of a village named Krishna Rakshit Chak in gram panchayat Arjun in Kharagpur block I of Midnapore district in West Bengal, India. As already mentioned in section 3.1, the village is poor and its villagers belong to the 'Lodha' tribe. The village has 49 households in 1993 as per the villagers, some of whom own small pieces of land distributed under the 'Operation Barga' programme of the state government.

This was our second visit to the village (the first visit being in February 1991) for a PRA session with the villagers on health. The villagers remembered interacting with us during '91 and doing a well-being grouping of households on a social map of the village. They expressed their joy at our re-visiting their village and sat together quite comfortably to do a mapping of the village without our asking for it. They brought some coloured sketch pens from their primary school and were looking for papers when we were able to actually offer them some sheets of paper. They started with a social map and explained various dimensions like literacy, male/female ratio and also identified the 'poorest of the poor'. We asked them about their health conditions and to show them household-wise on a village map. While the maps were in progress on one side of the primary school building the village women on the other side were preparing a seasonal food calendar to show the variations in their food intake.

The focus of the present section is on health PRA done by the villagers in the village Krishna Rakshit Chak. The main thrust of the health PRA was to learn about the health-status of the village community. The health mapping of the village Krishna Rakshit Chak was done by a group of villagers led by a primary school teacher of the village. The health map as given in Chart 30 shows different aspects of health of villagers such as those affected by diseases like polio, tuberculosis, leprosy, asthma and piles. In the area of family planning, the map shows those households which have adopted family planning, the number of pregnant women, lactating mothers and cases of abortion. The health map also shows old age as an aspect of health and those households having aged people in them.

Some of the features of village households as indicated in the health map are as follows:

(i) It gives a brief summary of diseases affecting individual households.

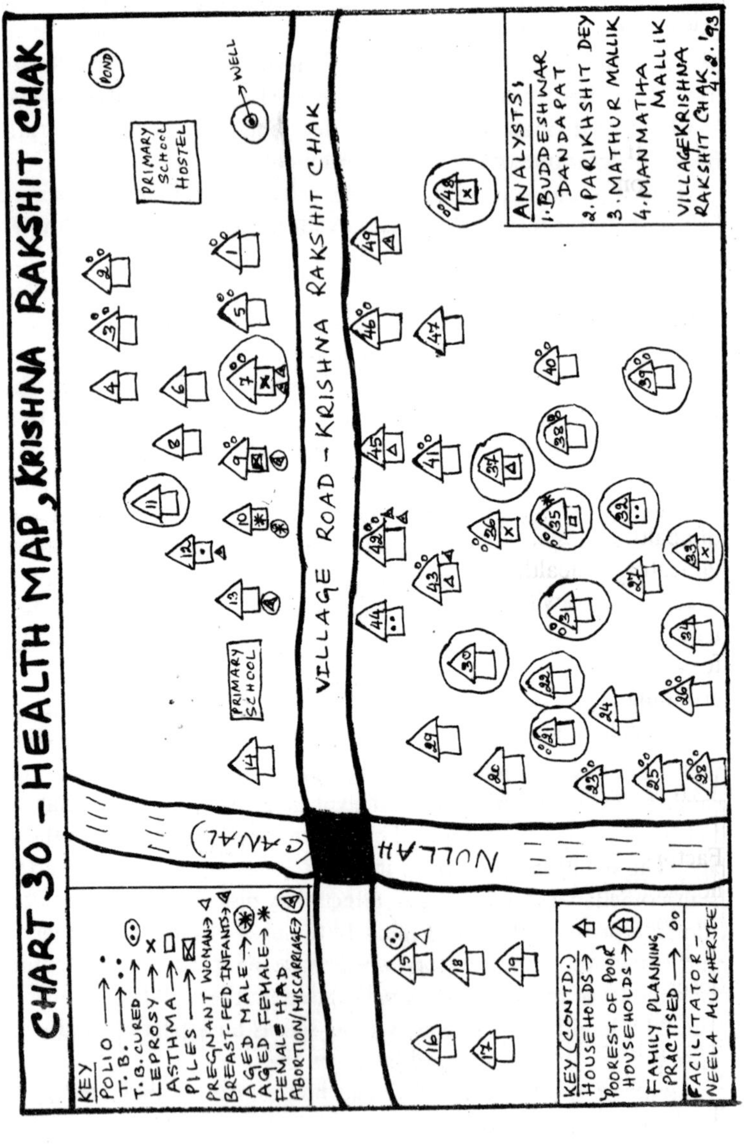
CHART 30 - HEALTH MAP, KRISHNA RAKSHIT CHAK
KEY
POLIO
T.B.
T.B. CURED
LEPROSY
ASTHMA
PILES
PREGNANT WOMAN
BREAST-FED INFANTS
AGED MALE
AGED FEMALE
FEMALE HAD ABORTION/MISCARRIAGE
CANAL
NULLAH
VILLAGE ROAD - KRISHNA RAKSHIT CHAK
PRIMARY SCHOOL
PRIMARY SCHOOL HOSTEL
WELL
POND
ANALYSTS:
1. BUDDESHWAR DANDAPAT
2. PARIKHSHIT DEY
3. MATHUR MALLIK
4. MANMATHA MALLIK
VILLAGE KRISHNA RAKSHIT CHAK 4.8.'93
KEY (CONTD.)
HOUSEHOLDS
POOREST OF POOR HOUSEHOLDS
FAMILY PLANNING PRACTISED
FACILITATOR - NEELA MUKHERJEE

(ii) There are 3 cases of piles, 4 cases of leprosy, 3 cases of tuberculosis of which one case was cured.
(iii) Ten women were lactating mothers out of a total of 68.
(iv) Twenty-two households had adopted family planning methods which was around 45 percent coverage of total households in the village.
(v) If one projects the social map of villagers on the health map one finds 13 households identified by the village group as 'poorest of the poor' of which 7 households or more than 50 percent have adopted family planning.
(vi) All the 4 cases of leprosy are to be found in the 'poorest of poor' households. The limited earning capacity of persons affected by leprosy is well understood. The social problems of a leprosy-ridden household is also not easy to resolve.
(vii) Incidence of TB, asthma and oldage, all exist in the 'poorest of the poor' households.

The health map, however, does not portray an important aspect of health and that is food-intake. This is all the more important as an indicator of health in a village where the villagers are poor and are required to go without proper food- intake periodically. This came to light through well-being grouping of households and the seasonal food calendar as done by the villagers. The details of well-being grouping and seasonal food calendar are presented in section 3.1 and section 3.2.

3.3.6 *Factors Determining State of Health*

Factors which determine state of health are very important for a health PRA. Much can be learnt from what villagers describe as factors leading to their ill health. This may or may not help in diagnosis of local factors causing certain kinds of illness. Often, the factors described by local people may not be the real factors but can help in indicating the cause of illness or in educating them. In a PRA conducted in a village in Muzaffarpur, Bihar, India, the villagers mentioned about many of them, both adult and child, affected by 'hydrocil'. They expressed their opinion that the quality of their village water had something to do with so many cases of 'hydrocil'. However, a medical opinion was slightly different. According to one medical opinion, it was filariasis which was prevalent in that area and caused secondary 'hydrocil'. It is not unnatural to expect large divergences in rural perceptions from established medical opinion. The illness described by rural communities can be mere symptoms. The medicines they take and their beliefs and practices can all be unscientific according to established medical opinion. However, in the first place, it is important to understand the merit of their argument and their perceptions in planning effective health interventions.

Food deficiency in a poor household can be a source of many problems including that of under-nourishment and mal-nourishment of children. This can be reflected through a food calendar showing periodic variations in food availability, kinds of food and food intake by selected households. For example, a medical opinion on the food calendar made by a group of rural women of Krishna Rakshit Chak, as shown in section 3.2, is that the diet of the villagers is grossly deficient in proteins and different kinds of vitamins. It is a highly imbalanced diet, possibly low in terms of calories (since absolute quantity of food is not indicated in the food calendar) and that consumption of pulses and green vegetables should go up in proportion to rice and potatoes so as to make for better health of the villagers. In this case, the revelation of the villagers about their seasonal variations in food intake made it possible for an examination of their food content from the point of food value.

With regard to the aspect of seeking treatment or going without proper treatment by rural people one can have many reasons. In field experience, we often find that many villagers do not undergo proper treatment on account of different reasons, amongst which are personal beliefs, treatment by 'quacks', lack of means of transport to carry sick people to the doctor, improper functioning of the health centres, inadequate follow up etc.

3.3.7 *Practice of Indigenous Medicines*

In rural areas use of indigenous treatment and medicines are generally quite common. In a PRA session with a tribe in a village, such indigenous treatment and medicines practised by them were brought to the fore. Such a PRA session was conducted in a village named Bhaniyawala in Doiwala block of Dehradun district in Uttar Pradesh, India. The tribe belongs to that of 'snake charmers'. Their livelihood is based on charming of snakes in public places and selling of indigenous medicines. By tradition, they sell medicines procured from medicinal plants and animals. In that PRA session with the villagers, different aspects of their procuring, recommending and selling of medicines were brought to light. On asking them the range of illness which they were able to cure, they said that they had medicines for almost all kinds of illness and spoke of different kinds of medicines which they knew and practised. They listed some of the illness and also the medicines they recommended. Some of them were as shown in Table 3.8.

TABLE 3.8: Illness and Indigenous Medicines

Illness	Medicines
(i) Cough and cold	'kaya manjan tej rasa'
(ii) Pneumonia	-do-
(iii) Liver disorders	-do-
(iv) Post-natal problems	-do-
(v) Eczema	'narbish'
(vi) Leukemia	through blowing of a special horn of an animal and through external application of a special medicine prepared from lime juice and kerosene oil
(vii) Rheumatism and muscular pain	through blowing of a special horn of an animal

They described the medicine of 'kaya manjan tej rasa' as being prepared from porcupine's liver extracts plus certain salts and seeds mixed together. The tribe in order to prepare medicines from animal extracts were required to kill foxes, rabbits, porcupines, mongoose and other animals. Such animals were not only used for medicines but also for their day to day food consumptions. Apart from consuming meat, the villagers also used the skins of the animals for making of some musical instruments to charm snakes.

In that PRA session it was felt that some villagers from the group were not willing to share many of their traditional medicines and practices for some reason or the other and were reluctant to continue with the list. Hence, the list mentions only a few illness and their treatment.

The villagers expressed their problems in procuring animals from the forests. They were facing difficulties in finding animals and plants due to strict forest laws. Instead, they were able to catch a few animals from the near-by fields owned by big landlords who were engaged in cultivation of sugarcane. They also mentioned that they often had to undertake journeys to remote corners of Himalayas to procure medicinal roots and plants.

3.3.8 *Some Reflections on Health PRA*

Health is wealth. Improvement in rural health conditions implies that the rural people can work more and earn more. With regard to indigenous and modern kinds of treatment for diseases, the villagers tend to exercise their own choice of the kind of treatment to avail. The choice depends on the type of treatment, its proximity, its cost, their beliefs and outlook. Whether it is for health awareness camps/programmes or functioning of rural health centres and health workers, it is important to learn about the local people's priorities, beliefs, attitudes and approaches to health-related issues.

Summary

Rural health is a complex subject and inter-related with many other aspects of rural life. It is a wide area in scope and content and hence, needs to be perceived in a larger context. This is because there are several factors which influence rural health and these in turn, lend their impact on the well-being of an individual, his household and the village community at large. Some of the illustrations in this section demonstrate that it has its connections with food, work, outlook, ecology, health services, cultural perceptions, indigenous vs. modern systems of medicines and other related factors. It is only through direct participation that one learns about the health status of rural people, the kinds of illness, their linkages, sources, origin, treatment and other aspects. Hence, direct participation has the potential of improving the efficiency of health services.

REFERENCES

Borrini, Grazia(ed.) (1991), *Lessons Learned in Community-based Environmental Management*, Proceedings of the 1990 Primary Environmental Care Workshop, International Course for Primary Health Care Managers at District Level in Developing Countries, Rome, April.

Dreze, Jean and Sen, Amartya (1990), *The Political Economy of Hunger*, vol.1, 2 & 3, Clarendon Press, Oxford.

Grosvenor-Alsop, Ruth (1989), 'Wealth ranking in a Caste Area of India', *RRA Notes,* Number 4, February, London.

Jodha, N. S., (1991), Rural Common Property Resources, A Growing Crisis, Gatekeeper Series no. 24, SA 10, Sustainable Agriculture Program, IIED,

London.

RRA Notes (1992), No. 16, IIED, London.

Sarkar, Anup (1991), 'Wealth Ranking in Mahilong, Bihar', *RRA Notes*, No.13, August.

Scoones, Ian (1992), Wealth Ranking: Insights into Patterns of Rural Differentiation in Southern Zimbabwe, typescript, Sustainable Agriculture Programme, IIED, London.

Sen, Amartya (1984), *Poverty and Famines, Essays in Entitlement and Deprivation*, Oxford University Press, Oxford.

Shah, Parmesh (1990), 'Economic Classification of a Community Using Locally Generated Criteria', *RRA Notes,* Number 8, IIED, London.

Smith, Shelia and Sender, John, (1988), 'Investigating Poverty: An Example from Tanzania', *RRA Notes*, Number 2, October, London.

TISS (1991 & 1992), *Qualitative Research Methods Newsletter,* Department of Health Services Studies, Tata Institute of Social Sciences, Bombay.

4

POLICY MEASURES, LIMITATIONS AND OPPORTUNITIES OF PRA

This is the last chapter of the present study. In this chapter we suggest selected policy measures, some limitations in the use of PRA, selected dimensions of PRA as a methodology and concluding remarks. The chapter starts with a description of a set of policy measures flowing from the case studies on poverty and well-being presented earlier in Chapter 3, section 3.1. It is an attempt to suggest some policy implications of the wealth-grouping performed by rural communities in terms of selected measures. The policy measures are, however, specific to the case studies of the villages concerned. While drawing policy implications we also compare such policy measures with the policies generally advocated in the conventional approach to poverty reduction.

4.1 Policy Measures from Rural Communities' Wealth-grouping

The two case studies of rural communities on wealth grouping presented in Chapter 3 can have two sets of policy measures, one, based on the conventional 'top-down' approach with income as a standard indicator of poverty and the other flowing from people's perceptions through PRA. In the conventional framework, the approach to poverty proceeds generally through assessing the income of households and classifying them into different groups. On the basis of income-based classification of households, the 'top-down' approach suggests income generation of poor households either through official wage employment generation programmes at a local level or through self-employment programmes at a household level such as running of small business, shops etc. by poor households.

The focus of income-based classification of households would logically recommend increase in income through income generation schemes. Any increase in income through such schemes whether through wage employment or through starting of household business can help in reducing the number of days of starvation for the villagers but would fail to influence the underlying forces responsible for poverty of the villagers. Generally, there is one-off creation of wage-employment opportunities such as building a school or a dispensary and this continues on a sporadic basis. Such an approach hardly helps in having a long-term view of endemic poverty. Whereas, self-employment opportunities in household business would have to be examined in the context of opportunities for those whose consumption requirements are of much greater priority than their investment requirements which means there is every possibility of depletion of investment capital of poor households for consumption purposes. In practice, a small number of households from the two villages described in Chapter 3, section 3.1, are beneficiaries of governmental programmes which are not only of minor consequence to the beneficiary households but also for the village as a whole.

Poverty reduction through income generation has failed to touch upon many dimensions of poverty without which attempts at reducing poverty are of limited use. These dimensions remain unperceived or under-perceived in the conventional approach. These relate to some of those aspects which were, directly revealed by rural communities of the two villages under discussion.

The results of the study of rural communities' perceptions need not have general applicability to other villages. Each village community has its own resource endowment, natural resource base, socio-economic features, problems, priorities and preferences. Their perceptions of poverty and well-being would depend on their perceptions of the relative importance of different factors. However, the results of the villagers' analysis through wealth grouping can give us some indication of immediate policy measures to be undertaken in the villages of Krishna Rakshit Chak and Kalsigeriya, under study.

First, it helps us in understanding trends in rural areas. These findings indicate decreasing well-being on many counts such as decline in food availability and increase in hunger, diminished accessibility to common property resources and shrinking choice. Although psychologically, well-being has been augmented through possession of land holdings through land reforms, the degradation of common property resources has far outweighed such a benefit directly affecting food availability, accentuating starvation and indirectly restricting choices. Environmental degradation has been so rapid and widespread that it threatens the very basis of quality of life of rural poor.

Based on rural communities' perceptions of poverty and well-being a package of policy measures can be suggested which incorporates food security for poor households, regeneration and management of common property resources, special support to single widowed households, increased employment opportunities and other supportive measures.

4.1.1 *Food Security*

Rural people's perceptions indicate, that, since the incidence of starvation has increased in the villages described above, the villagers require immediate food security whether through free ration or food for work programmes. The villages are semi-starved and 'food for work' programmes can be introduced on an appropriate scale during the lean seasons so as to prevent mass hunger and starvation. The programmes can be more specific by concentrating on those months in which the villagers are worst affected in terms of food availability. Based on their own 'food calendar' which describes the availability of food in different months and seasons there can be a basis for public intervention for increasing the total availability of food depending on the deficit in the village from time to time. A food calendar has been described in Chapter 3, section 3.2, where the village women of Krishna Rakshit Chak have prepared such a calendar to show their seasonal food variations.

4.1.2 *Upliftment of Rural Widows*

Rural communities' ranking of poor households as in the village of Kalsigeriya indicate that the group constituting 'poorest of the poor' include many widows. The deprivation of rural widows is widely known and has many causes related to their deprivation with regard to residence, inheritance, remarriage, employment and community support. These would however, vary extensively within regions and in communities within the same region (Dreze:1990). Widowhood enhances a woman's vulnerability, deprivation and poverty. There is a need for public intervention in order to approach the socio-economic problems of widows. The immediate requirement is for public support towards protecting their living standards with direct transfers from state in cash or kind. Other measures which can be of assistance to widows are special programmes for betterment of their economic livelihood and their increased access to facilities for betterment of their education and health.

4.1.3 *Regeneration of Environmental Resources*

As per villagers' perceptions, common property resources play an important role in the life of rural poor. When degradation of such resources is on the rise, as shown in the villages under discussion, there is an urgency to find ways of maintaining and increasing their benefits to rural people. One way is that of community initiative for regeneration, maintenance and preservation of common property resources. Community participation in development efforts can be based on joint planning and decision-making. This, if indigenously based, would be more realistic and acceptable than that done exogenously by outside agencies. PRA can be used as a method for mobilising rural community as well as to monitor the status and upkeep of common property resources.

The first step towards natural resource management for sustainable development of these semi-starved villages lies in direct interaction between village community and policy-makers, administrators, planners, extension workers and scientists. It is important to learn of rural communities' indigenous knowledge system related to their socio-economic and ecological variables affecting their quality of life and also the scope for such a system to rectify degraded livelihoods. On the other hand, it is also important to know the kind of external support plausible and available in terms of financial resources and scientific knowledge and technologies to tackle local problems. The two sides can then be matched for sustainable livelihoods.

There are a known range of technologies to enhance yields and reduce environmental contamination having the potential to increase private returns and reducing both private and social costs (Pretty:1990). Further environmental degradation of the villages can be prevented based on local knowledge, community participation and external support for accessibility to financial resources and environmentally-sound technologies. On such a basis, a reversal can be initiated towards enrichment or depauperisation of the villages. Technologies appropriate to the villages can be adopted for an integrated approach encompassing agro-forestry, pest management, nutrient conservation and soil and water conservation.

4.1.4 *Community Involvement and Empowerment*

The villagers can organise themselves for community action. Community involvement builds upon sustainable use of local resources and strengthens community self-reliance. Community empowerment would enhance their level of involvement in the development process. It can liberate the energy of the community to work, innovate and diversify its livelihood base. Community-based projects show high levels of cost recovery, project effectiveness and efficiency in use of resources and expansion of productive resource base at low levels of per capita investment (Borrini:1991).

Community involvement however, is a slow and a complex process. Constraints to such involvement can be in the form of lack of capital, information, expertise and managerial resources (Borrini:1991). There is also scope for conflicts to arise in establishing priorities for action and opposition of groups with vested interests can distort total community welfare. But community involvement is an exercise in 'learning by doing' for the community and development agencies and depends on the gains perceived through such action. The net effects of involvement in most areas are expected to increase total community welfare and state interventions and interventions by non-governmental development organisations can also play a powerful role in creating a congenial framework so as to facilitate community empowerment in socio-political terms.

4.1.5 *Sustainable Agriculture*

The rural communities under study are bearing the social costs of agricultural pollution which have degraded their common property resources like ponds and forests. The traditional mixed farming system was sustainable. It generated few adverse social impact and used lesser quantity of external resources. With the onset of Green Revolution, the goal of increased productivity of agriculture was achieved by introduction of modern varieties of crops augmented by use of fertilisers and pesticides. Intensification of agriculture has brought new practices leading to greater chemical use which has increased the pollution of environment. In many countries over-use of agro-chemicals arises because of low costs relative to other inputs (Pretty:1990).

Over-use of fertilizers can give rise to entrophication of rivers, lakes and coastal waters that can cause environmental harm. Nitrate and phosphate in rivers and lakes can also lead to dense algal growth causing loss of aquatic plants, losses of fish and acquatic life (Conway and Pretty:1991).

Agricultural activities outside village have created extensive pollution of sources of water in the villages for instance, in Krishna Rakshit Chak and in Kalsigeriya, which has affected the livelihood of rural poor. Attempts to reduce the social costs of pollution require effective state intervention apart from community involvement. State action is required to clean the water sources from pollution which has already taken place and the treatment of water can be a costly affair. The state policies towards fertilisers and pesticides have also to be redesigned so as to prevent their excessive-use, reduce the divergence between private costs of using fertilizers and pesticides and social costs of agriculture pollution and encourage use of local resources and traditional knowledge systems.

Community empowerment can play a powerful role in creating a sustainable system of agriculture, by use of local resources, lower dependence on external inputs and adopt agro-ecological technologies which are environment-friendly (Pretty *et al.*:1992). Based on the village experiences, it can be observed that it is essential to set rural development into an ecological framework. This, however, is not enough by itself. The active involvement of the concerned communities is also a pre-condition for sustainability of any intervention. Community participation can describe local developmental problems and can reflect on the identification of risks, resources and opportunities for local development. The community can work towards making programmes sustainable and environmentally compatible.

If villagers' criteria of well-being do not match with that of outside agencies like those of the governmental or non-governmental organizations then interventions for rural development is not as efficient as desired and, is generally, not able to deliver the expected results. The greater the divergence between community's perceptions of well-being and that of outside agencies the less relevant becomes the efforts of the latter. Hence, as a policy issue, it is critical to know how people evaluate their quality of life and what criteria they actually use for doing so. For this purpose it is important to facilitate rural communities/groups/individuals to come up with their criteria of well-being. Such participation can increase the effectiveness of the programmes by designing them, monitoring them and evaluating them.

The application of PRA tools in facilitation of rural communities' perception of poverty and well-being in selected Indian villages clearly demonstrate that such tools can unfold villagers' perceptions in capturing the different dimensions of poverty and well-being and grouping of households on that basis. As a policy-tool, PRA can be effective in generating indicators of well-being and also in facilitating community participation for designing and implementation of suitable programmes for improvement of rural quality of life.

4.2 Limitations of PRA as a Methodology

In this section, we discuss some of the weaknesses of PRA and the limitations posed to the use of PRA as a methodology. No methodology is all-perfect and PRA is no exception to this general rule. PRA, alike other methodologies, has its own share of imperfections. The relevant issue in this context is first, what kind and how big are the imperfections and second, can they be overcome or minimised ? Much depends on what the imperfections are and whether there are ways to bring the imperfections within reasonable limits in order to have better results from rural participation.

Each PRA exercise is unique in its own way. In each case, it starts in its own manner and proceeds in its own style based on the principles of PRA and there can be no 'blue-print' recommended for a PRA session. The amount of learning which takes place in a PRA exercise and the data generated can vary from situation to situation.

4.2.1 *Changing Attitudes*

The problem starts from changing of attitudes towards rural people in order to be willing to learn from them and to appreciate the importance of their participation in decision-making. This, however, is not easily done. In many cases, attitudinal changes about rural people and their capabilities can be brought about through training and observing PRA sessions in field-oriented situations. Bringing about attitudinal changes for large bureaucracies is a mammoth task and requires training of numerous functionaries in government and non-government organisations. This itself is time-consuming and resource-intensive.

4.2.2 *'Rapidity' and Cultural Dimensions*

Some anthropologists tend to believe that semi-structured interviews are one-off attempts to capture 'real' life worlds at the local levels which need not be realistic. They hold the view that there are no short-cut ways for learning about a given culture. According to them an understanding of rural realities is time-consuming and involves learning of local language, culture and gradually making ones physical presence unobstrusive. Learning a culture – its subtleties, sensitiveness and other details are against rapidity. At best, rapid appraisals can be polite conversations (Pottier:1991).

Only long-term fieldwork can make an anthropologist competent for assessing the circumstances under which interviews can take place. Long term residence and language familiarity can check the danger of significant bias creeping into interviews. To gain from an interview, a researcher must understand the participants' modes of thought, their socially constructed values, their attitudes towards interviews, their ways of manipulating interviews and others. Insights into all such areas can be gained only from long-term fieldwork (Pottier:1991).

In this context, it is worth arguing that to be realistic, there is a need for a method which is able to generate relevant data in comparatively less time than long-term anthropological studies and is also relatively quicker than sample surveys. And it is here that PRA fits well with such a requirement.

4.2.3 *'Rapidity' and Reality*

This is a criticism associated with the feature of rapid data collection of methods like PRA. Some doubts have been raised whether methods involving 'rapid appraisal' are appropriate for understanding contemporary social change. Some have expressed concern that the practice of rapid appraisal can become popular because of its rapid results and can be frequently used so as to go out of control (Pottier: 1991).

It is thought that PRA can help in quick access to indigenous world (e.g., technical knowledge, rural perceptions, decision-making). The basic idea is that "the data are out there to be collected, objectively and quickly" (Pottier:1991) and this can be done by asking rural people and using some common sense. The presumption of PRA is that friendly interaction can bring out rural people's knowledge and perceptions. However, critics are of the opinion that the scope for discrepancy between response of informants and what they actually do or think may be quite different and this cannot be comprehended by outsiders without entering into a discourse of a given culture, not rapid but a slow and painful approach (Pottier:1991).

There is some truth in the above argument but the context in which PRA is being emphasised is quite different. The 'rapid' feature of PRA needs to be appreciated in comparison to a method like that of a survey questionnaire which is an accepted method for official data collection. It is in this context, that the relatively 'quick' and participatory nature of PRA would yield better quality of information which is cost-effective as well. Sessions of PRA can extend over several days depending on the topic concerned and the emphasis in PRA in more on 'participation' rather than on 'rapidity'.

4.2.4 *Relevance of Visual Methods*

It is said that visual representations which are integral to PRA can be alien to many societies and hence the responses, comments and interpretations of the representations may not be the same which the researchers think they are getting. Apart from this issue it has been argued by a group of 'slow researchers and practitioners' in U.K. that some methods of PRA are of not of any practical use. For instance, the method of venn diagramming is not of any use to villagers since it is a descriptive way to show interactions or lack of the same between institutions/individuals. It does not help in analysing how institutional problems can be resolved.

In answer to the points raised above, it may be said that visual representations make points simple to understand and provide a tangible base for discussion. The PRA team members can take care of the discrepancies in rural perceptions and their interpretations through relevant discussions, use of different methods and other sources of rural knowledge. As for venn diagrams the presentations of interactions and relationships of individuals/institutions are themselves important in understanding of rural realities. They project the state of the relationships and unless one knows such a state one is unable to learn further in this direction. Analysis of such relationships and bringing about changes in them constitute separate issues.

4.2.5 *Not Always Easy to Conduct*

There are many variables influencing a participatory process and attempts at conducting a PRA need not result in having an effective

PRA session. Sometimes a PRA may not even happen or it may take unduly long to happen. It may not be possible to initiate a PRA exercise for reasons more than one. One reason of such a situation may be due to problems in the behaviour of outsiders while another reason may be that the people are not willing to participate for lack of time or some other factor. On many occasions, they may not wish to participate and share their perceptions. In such cases, one need not be unnecessarily pessimistic and should not give up easily. On such occasions, it is important to remember that there can be different experiences and large variations in attempts at initiating villagers to PRA. There are no clear-cut ways which can help in ensuring participation. Each PRA exercise is a process of learning for the 'outsider'. We have shown earlier, with an illustration in chapter 1, that even with friendly behaviour the villagers can feel withdrawn and inhibited. The poor villagers tend to be elusive which makes a PRA exercise all the more challenging.

4.2.6 *People's Expectations*

A PRA can be conducted in such a manner that it raises expectations of positive things to happen. If expectations are unnecessarily raised and not followed up in due course the situation can turn to be problematic. Hence, it is essential, that at all times, the objective of a PRA exercise should be explained to the rural people and on that basis their voluntary participation can be solicited. For instance, if a PRA exercise is for the sake of training of outsiders or for the purpose of research then the same is to be explained to the rural community, whose participation is being sought.

Development agencies, conducting PRA, should exercise caution in not raising expectations which they would find difficult to fulfil. People can easily get frustrated when they spend their time, do their own analysis but no change takes place and status quo is maintained (Action Aid-Ethiopia/IIED :1989). In case expectations are raised then genuine attempts at fulfilling such expectations would help rural people to have faith in development strategy and process.

4.2.7 *More Precision in Assigning Responsibilities*

In a village planning process through PRA, experience (Ford & Lelo:1991) shows that precision is required in assigning responsibilities for different kinds of work to be done including finding of those people who will be responsible for finding external inputs such as funds, building materials etc. Ways to find external resources by rural people for project implementation through PRA is also not easy. This may mean approaching the government, NGOs or donor agencies by rural communities for external inputs. It is pointed out that the community leaders often lack the skills to use PRA data for formulating project proposals and procuring external funds (Ford & Lelo:1991). Hence even when villagers do their own PRA they face difficulties in implementing their own plans and programmes. This indicates that support by development agencies in implementation of village plans through PRA is a critical input in the process of development.

4.2.8 *PRA and Sensitive Issues*

Sensitive issues need to be handled carefully in a PRA exercise. Surfacing of such issues through PRA can, at times, increase tensions and lead to difficult situations. The opinions expressed by one group may clash with those expressed by another group in heterogenous communities with large socio-economic and political differences. One example of sensitive issues can be communal feelings in stratified societies which need to be handled carefully for they can create problems for PRA sessions.

On many occasions, a PRA exercise can be used in a constructive manner for conflict resolution of different problems facing rural communities. An important determinant of which is the team which conducts the PRA and the key informants associated with a PRA exercise. Their ability to handle an issue in a positive manner can resolve conflicts and diffuse explosive situations. At all stages, however, the cooperation and participation of rural communities are essential requirements.

4.2.9 *Enthusiasm can Die Easily*

After conducting an initial PRA, sustaining the enthusiasm of local people for implementation of their own plans can sometimes pose to be problematic. It has been experienced that initial enthusiasm is high as a result of PRA but easily withers off after some months. PRA teams can attend to long-term mobilisation of community (Ford & Lelo:1991). Hence, good facilitators are important for sustaining the interest of local people.

4.2.10 *People's Empowerment and Participation-friendly Environment*

PRA does not go well with every institutional framework. PRA is people's empowerment which need not fit with the socio-political parameters existing in institutions of many countries and regions. PRA may not be meaningful in repressive conditions. In such conditions, people may not be willing to reveal their perceptions or tell the truth. This, however, is not a weakness which is inherent in PRA. It calls for greater democratization of development. An ideal institutional setting for PRA is one which is congenial to participation, a setting which is not only open but one in which there is provision for decision-making to start from the bottom.

4.2.11 *No final answer*

No method can promise to guarantee a final answer. The same is with PRA which is not expected to provide final solutions to rural problems. It should be looked upon as an approach towards better understanding of rural problems, rural views and preferences rather than providing final answers. Some rural problems are too complex to be dealt with at the local level and resolving of such problems may become difficult even with a PRA focusing on them. However, such a PRA exercise can also make an useful contribution towards problem-solving.

PRA induces participation and brings forth indigenous knowledge and involvement of local people. These are considered to be essential inputs in search for improved solutions. The views and opinions of the rural people can give indications of their possible involvement, the limitations of their indigenous solutions and the extent to which they would participate in approaching a problem. These are far more important as initial steps to approaching rural problems rather than having rural communities sitting as passive onlookers of development programmes.

4.2.12 *Training and its Scale*

PRA can fail to give its best results if the team members are not trained properly. They may be inexperienced or unskilled with difficult attitudes and may have a tendency to rush the process (Messerschmidt:1991) and hence, proper training is an essential component of PRA. PRA team members need training in the right kind of approach, to initiate participation, use of methods, facilitation and analysis of data generated. Greater the speed at which PRA spreads, greater is the need for trainers conducting training at different levels.

Experience shows that at the village level, it is important to create an inventory of local leaders who are capable of organizing community participation. They can facilitate the PRA planning process starting from data collection to implementation (Ford & Lelo:1991).

PRA is a powerful methodology for rural development and it is important that its limitations are recognised and understood so as to use PRA for bringing about maximum benefit to the society. It is important to remember that PRA is not a final answer to rural development, it is rather an approach to seek an answer. It is a flexible methodology which incorporates a host of methods which, both directly and indirectly support rural learning. For e.g., secondary data review from conventional methods help PRA teams in doing their groundwork and having background materials. Apart from quantitative data through different methods, the strength of PRA lies in generation of qualitative data which numerical measures are not capable of reflecting. PRA encourages participation between outsiders and rural people as well as within rural people themselves.

4.3 Selected Dimensions of PRA

In this section, we have described selected dimensions of PRA which bring out its role as a methodology for generation of information and strengthening and expanding of information base for rural development.

4.3.1 *Nature and Kind of Data Through PRA*

Data generated through PRA can be both qualitative and quantitative. The main objective of PRA methods is to understand the perspective of others. The perspective can be expression of rural people's perceptions both in quantitative or numerical terms and/or in qualitative terms. A person whose perceptions are being sought requires enough flexibility to articulate his or her responses in the way he or she wishes to. It can be centered on a problem, a comparative evaluation of issues or ranking of priorities and preferences or enumerating problems and suggesting solutions. Such expression of views can be through objects, figures, comparisons or in any other form. The strength of PRA lies in its flexibility of generating both quantitative and qualitative data through a range of methods appropriate for revealing rural people's perceptions.

4.3.2 *Period of Data*

PRA methods can help to generate data both at a point of time for example, data on health status of a village on a particular date and also over a period of time, extending over a couple of years for e.g., physical changes in village or changes in wage rate of agricultural labourers over a period of time. PRA can also account for data relating to changes on an annual basis such as crop production or rainfall pattern. Data through PRA can also be seasonal, pertaining to seasonal food availability or seasonal work load of rural women.

4.3.3 *Scale of Data*

Data generated through PRA can be for a person, household, village or group of villages. In this case, the objective pursued is important for the size and kind of data required. Through PRA sessions one can find trends and patterns or the analysis of difference existing in rural communities. PRA data across villages can give broad indications of patterns if any. However, PRA's major strength lies in the analysis of difference.

4.3.4 *PRA in Complementing Questionnaire-survey*

As compared to the survey method, PRA is a method which is neither looking for 'averages' nor for set patterns. It has a range of methods primarily for analysis of differences in rural phenomena and processes. It is based on people's perceptions to analyse the complexities and heterogeneity underlying rural systems and processes. It may be argued against PRA that lack of standardization in the concepts and categories emerging from PRA can make comparability difficult across areas and over time. In this case, it is important to mention that if PRA is looking at rural processes and phenomena many of which cannot be standardised then the question of standardisation for the sake of comparability does not arise. It can also be argued against PRA that such a method can give undue attention to dramatic events or changes in the 'outliers' rather than to the central tendency. The answer is that the problem of poverty is such that the events or changes away from the central tendency are more important and play a major role in explaining it. In this context, there lies great scope for both survey methods and PRA methods to complement each other in building up a rich rural information base.

4.3.5 *Statistical Tools and PRA*

The scope for the use of statistical tools in PRA data depends on the kind of data available. Statistical tools based on averages may not always be relevant for data analysis especially when the information generated through PRA is of a qualitative nature. However, to the quantitative data generated by PRA one can even fit regression equations over time or across households/villages and also use 'dummy' variables for gaining an 'average' picture of the issue at hand.

4.3.6 *Duration of PRA*

Learning from villagers can be relatively quick if proper environment for participation prevails. A map of a village can take between an hour to half a day or still more following which interviews can be conducted for analysis of the map. The duration of a PRA session depends on the size of the village and aspects to be covered. The diverse are the aspects of learning involved the more time it takes. In case of difficulties in rapport-building with rural people the time taken for a PRA session can be longer for proper learning to take place.

4.3.7 *Villagers' Analysis through PRA*

Analysis by rural people can be short or long, qualitative or quantitative and simple or complicated. It can be analysis through narration or by means of other methods. The performer is important and validation of the data generated is also important. The analysis can be by communities, groups and individuals. Some villagers are better and quicker than others in analysing and revealing their perceptions.

4.3.8 *Whose Perceptions and Reality?*

The main objective of PRA as a methodology is to understand the perspectives of the rural people and not to proceed with preconceived sets of ideas and notions. A PRA team applies PRA methods to find the perceptions of the rural people in latter's framework for understanding of rural phenomena. It is important that outsiders are willing to learn, have respect for rural people and facilitate them so that their rural perceptions are revealed.

4.3.9 *Element of Openness*

PRA methods are based on the element of openness where the researcher acts as a facilitator to the villagers' perceptions to open up their discussions and views so as to interact from within, in natural surroundings. The methods help to establish effective communication with rural people. Communication is not only an instrument to learn about expressions, giving information but also an instrument of clarification of the importance of those expressions for the speaker (Streiffeler:1991). This aspect of openness in PRA needs to be emphasised because most methods, by nature are extractive rather than participatory including Rapid Rural Appraisal which is a forerunner of PRA. The extractive methods are based more on interpretations and understanding of outsiders rather than those of the participants.

4.4 Reflections on PRA

PRA has not evolved in scientific laboratories nor in intellectual writings but in field situations. This can be considered as a major strength of PRA in facing rural realities and it is this which has propelled a methodology like PRA to move forward and gain steadily from field experiences. This has also helped to make it innovative and open.

Many of the PRA methods are relatively new and still in the initial stages of development. Their experimentation and application have been in selected areas of rural life in selected countries. There is no upper limit to the whole range of methods which can evolve in the process of involving rural masses. PRA has a rich potential and offers a methodologically powerful opportunity of which development practitioners can make good use (Mukherjee:1991).

PRA, as a methodology, enjoys wide flexibility in terms of inducing participation in different institutional settings. In some restricted environments not conducive to participation. PRA can be used as a method for data collection. While, in other settings, congenial to participation, PRA can be used for decision making, implementation, monitoring and evaluation of developmental projects. Its role depends on the use to which it is put.

PRA derives its strength from the participative elements inherent in it which is the propelling force of PRA. It implies empowerment of people through active participation. It also implies realisation of self-worth and dignity of rural people, especially the poor and the weak. This can generate the confidence in capabilities of rural people and their self-learning. The goal of socio-economic development is attainment of well-being of every individual in a society. PRA provides an avenue for participation towards attainment of that well-being. It provides an enriched opportunity to initiate and sustain people's own development, planned, executed and evaluated by them.

Summary

In this chapter, we have discussed the major policy measures flowing from the case studies on poverty and well-being in Chapter 3, section 3.1. The policy measures arise out of rural communities' perceptions of poverty and have different dimensions in terms of food security, upliftment of rural widows, regeneration of environmental resources, community involvement and empowerment and sustainable agriculture.

PRA as a methodology is not without its limits. Some of its limitations like changing of attitudes, problems of rapidity, cultural context of diagramming, problems in conducting PRA, raising people's expectations, sensitivity of issues, lack of enthusiasm etc. can pose as problems in its use. However, the chapter also discusses how and to what extent the limitations of PRA can be overcome.

Towards the end, Chapter 4 discusses selected dimensions of PRA relating to the nature, kind, scale and period of data which PRA can generate and its role in complementing questionnaire-surveys. The chapter ends with a positive note on how PRA as a methodology can provide an enriched opportunity to initiate and sustain people's own development.

REFERENCES

Action Aid-Ethiopia/IIED (1989), *Action Aid in Local Partnership, an Experiment with Rapid Rural Appraisal in Ethiopia*, Sustainable Agriculture Programme, International Institute for Environment and Development, London.

Borrini, Grazia(ed.) (1991), *Lessons Learned in Community-based Environmental Management*, Proceedings of the 1990 Primary Environmental Care Workshop, International Course for Primary Health Care Managers at District Level in Developing Countries, Rome, April.

Conway, Gordon R. and Pretty, Jules (1991), *Unwelcome Harvest,* Earthscan, London.

Dreze, Jean (1990), *Widows in Rural India,* The Development Economics Research Programme, STICERD, London School of Economics, No.26, August.

Ford, Richard and Lelo, Francis (1991), 'Evaluating participatory rural appraisal: Listening to Village Leaders in Kakuyuni Location', *Forests, Trees and People Newsletter* No.13, June.

Group of 'slow' researchers and practitioners,'Can Rural Appraisal Really Be Rapid?', a critical assessment, typescript, U.K.

Messerschmidt, Donald A. (1991), *Rapid Appraisal For Community Forestry: The RA Process and Rapid Diagnostic Tools,* Institute of Forestry Project Technical Paper No. TP 91/2, IOF Project, Pokhara, Nepal.

Mukherjee, Neela (1991), 'An Alternative Approach to Rural Development- Participatory Rural Appraisal', in Yugandhar B.N. and Mukherjee Neela (ed.), *Studies in Village India*, Concept Publishing Company, Delhi.

Pottier, Johan (1991), 'Representation and Accountability: Understanding Social Change Through Rapid Appraisal, with reference to Northern Zambia', typescript, Department of Social Anthropology, S.O.A.S., University of London, April.

Pretty, Jules N. (1990), 'Agricultural Pollution: From Costs and Causes to Sustainable Practices', in Angell David J. R., Comer J. D., Wilkinson Mathew L. N.,(ed.), *Sustaining Earth*, Macmillan, London.

Pretty, Jules, Guijt, Irene, Scoones, Ian and Thompson, John (1992), 'Regenerating Agriculture: The Agroecology of Low External Input and Community-based Development' in Holmberg Johan(ed.), *Policies for a Small Planet,* From the International Institute for Environment and Development, Earthscan, London.

BIBLIOGRAPHY

Action Aid-Ethiopia/IIED, (1989), *Action Aid in Local Partnership, an Experiment with Rapid Rural Appraisal in Ethiopia*, Sustainable Agriculture Programme, International Institute for Environment and Development, London.

Borrini, Grazia (ed.), (1991), *Lessons Learned in Community-based Environmental Management*, Proceedings of the 1990 Primary Environmental Care Workshop, International Course for Primary Health Care Managers at District Level in Developing Countries, Rome, April.

Burgess, Robert G., (1990), *In the Field, An Introduction to Field Research, Contemporary Social Research Series*, General Editor: Martin Bulmer, Routledge, London.

Chambers, Robert, (1981), 'Rapid Rural Appraisal: Rationale and Repertoire', *IDS Discussion Paper No. 155*, IDS, Sussex.

Chambers, Robert, (1991a), 'In Search of Professionalism, Bureaucracy and Sustainable Livelihoods for the 21st Century', Typescript, I.D.S. Sussex, 28th May.

Chambers, Robert, (1991b), 'Shortcut and Participatory Methods for Gaining Social Information for Projects', in Cernea, Michael, M. (ed.), *Putting People First, Sociological Variables in Rural Development*, published for the World Bank, Oxford University Press.

Chambers, Robert, (1992), Rural Appraisal: Rapid, Relaxed and Participatory, *Discussion Paper 311*, Institute of Development Studies, October, Sussex.

Conway, G.R., (1985), Agroecosystem Analysis, *Agricultural Administration*, 20(1), 31.

Conway, G.R., (1986), *Agroecosystem Analysis for Research and Development*, Winrock International Institute for Agricultural Development, Bangkok, Thailand.

Conway, G.R., Mian, A., Alam, Z., Yar, M., and Husain, T., (1987), *Agroecosystem Zoning of the Hunza Valley: First Iteration*, May 1987, Draft Report, International Institute for Environment and

Development, London.

Conway, Gordan, (1988), 'Editorial – What's in a name', *RRA Notes* No.1, June.

Conway, Gordan R. and Pretty, Jules, (1991), *Unwelcome Harvest*, Earthscan, London.

Collinson, M.P., (1981), 'The Exploratory Survey Content, Methods and Detailed Guidelines, for Discussions with farmers', in *CIMMYT Eastern Africa Economic Programme Farming Systems Newsletter*, April-June.

Dewees, Peter, (1989), 'Aerial Photography and Household Studies in Kenya', *RRA Notes*, Number 7, September, IIED, London.

Dreze, Jean & Sen, Amartya, (1990), *The Political Economy of Hunger*, Vol. 1, 2 & 3, Clarendon Press, Oxford.

Dreze, Jean, (1990), *Widows in Rural India*, The Development Economics Research Programme, STICERD, London School of Economics, No. 26, August.

Ford, Richard and Lelo, Francis, (1991), 'Evaluating participatory rural appraisal: Listening to Village Leaders in Kakuyuni Location', *Forests, Trees and People, Newsletter* No. 13, June.

Grandin, Barbara, (1988), *Wealth Ranking in Smallholder Communities: a field manual*, Intermediate Technology Publications, London.

Grosvenor-Alsop, Ruth, (1989), 'Wealth ranking in a Caste Area of India', *RRA Notes*, Number 4, February, London.

Group of 'slow' researchers and practitioners, 'Can Rural Appraisal Really Be Rapid?' a critical assessment, typescript, U.K.

Guijt, Irene & Pretty, Jules, (1992), *Participatory Rural Appraisal for Farmer Participatory Research in Punjab, Pakistan*, IIED, London.

Hilderbrand, P.E., (1981), Combining disciplines in Rapid Appraisal: The Sondeo Approach, *Agricultural Administration*, 8(6), 423.

Jayakaran, Ravi, (1991), 'PRA Camp at Mahilong, Bihar, 27-30, November 11990: Krishi Gram Vikas Kendra', *RRA Notes*, Number 13, August, IIED, London.

Jodha, N.S., (1989), 'Social Science Research on Rural Change: Some Gaps', in Bardhan, Pranab, (ed.), *Conversations between Economists and Anthropologists*, Oxford University Press, Oxford.

Jodha, N.S., (1991), *Rural Common Property Resources, A Growing Crisis*, Gatekeeper Series no. 24, SA 19, Sustainable Agriculture Program, IIED, London.

Khon Kaen University, (1987), *Proceedings of 1985 International Conference on Rapid Rural Appraisal*, Rural Systems Research and Farming Systems Research Projects, Khon Kaen University, Khon Kaen, Thailand.

Kumar, Somesh and Kumari, Santhi A., (1991), "The Thippapur Experience: A PRA Diary", *RRA Notes* No. 11, December.

Lewis, W. Arthur, (1955), *The Theory of Economic Growth*, Homewood, Richard D. Irwin, Illinois.

Mascarenhas, Jimmy & Prem Kumar, P.D., (1991), 'Participatory Mapping and Modelling: Users' Notes', *RRA Notes*, Number 12, July, IIED, London.

Mathema, S.B. and Galt, D.L., (1987), 'The Samuhik Brahman Process in Nepal: A Multidisciplinary Group Activity to Approach Farmers', Paper presented at the *Workshop on Farmers and Agricultural Research: Complementary Methods*, Institute of Development Studies, England 26-31 July.

McCracken, Jennifer A., Pretty, Jules N. & Conway, Gordan R., (1988), *An Introduction to Rapid Rural Appraisal for Agricultural Development*, Sustainable Agriculture Programme, IIED, London.

McCracken, Jennifer, (1989), 'Diagrams for Participatory RRA', *RRA Notes*, September, IIED, London.

Mearns, Robin, (1988), 'On Oral History and Local Calendars: Experiences in the field in Papua New Guinea', *RRA Notes* Number 3, IIED, London.

Mearns, Robin, (1989), 'Aerial Photographs in Rapid Land Resource Appraisal, Papua New Guinea', *RRA Notes*, Number 7, September, IIED, London.

Messerschmidt, Donald A., (1991), Rapid Appraisal for Community Forestry: The RA Process and Rapid Diagnostic Tools, *Institute of Forestry Project Technical Paper* No. TP 91/2, IOF Project, Pokhara, Nepal.

Mukherjee, Neela, (1991), 'An Alternative Approach to Rural Development — Participatory Rural Appraisal', in Yugandhar, B.N. and Mukherjee, Neela (ed.), *Studies in Village India*, Concept Publishing Company, Delhi.

Mukherjee, Neela, (1992), 'Villagers' Perceptions of Rural Poverty through the Mapping method of PRA', *RRA Notes* No. 15, IIED, London.

Pottier, Johan, (1991), 'Representation and Accountability: Understanding Social Change through Rapid Appraisal, with reference to Northern Zambia', typescript, Department of Social Anthropology, S.O.A.S., University of London, April.

Pretty, Jules, (1988), 'Portraits and Stories', *RRA Notes* Number 3, IIED, London.

Pretty, Jules N., (1990), 'Agricultural Pollution: From Costs and Causes to Sustainable Practices', in Angell, David J.R., Comer, J.D. and Wilkinson, Mathew L.N. (ed.), *Sustaining Earth,* Macmillan, London.

Pretty, Jules, Guijt, Irene, Scoones, Ian and Thompson, John, (1992), 'Regenerating Agriculture: The Agroecology of Low External Input and Community-based Development' in Holmberg, Johan (ed.), *Policies for a Small Planet*, From the International Institute for Environment and Development, Earthscan, London.

Raintree, J.B. and Young, A., (1983), Guidelines for Agroforestry Diagnosis and Design, *ICRAF Working Paper* No. 6, Nairobi.

Rhoades, R.E., (1982), *The Art of the Informal Agricultural Survey,* International Potato Centre, Lima.

Rhoades, Robert E., (1987), 'Basic Field Techniques for Rapid Rural Appraisal', *Proceedings of 1985 International Conference on Rapid Rural Appraisal,* Rural Systems Research and Farming Systems Research Projects, Kohn Kaen University, Khon Kaen, Thailand.

RRA Notes, (1991), Number 13, August, IIED, London.

RRA Notes, (1992), Number 16, IIED, London.

Sandford, Dick, (1989), 'A Note on the Use of Aerial Photographs for Landuse Planning on a Settlement Site ion Ethiopia', *RRA Notes* Number 6, IIED, June.

Sarkar, Anup, (1991), 'Wealth Ranking in Mahilong', Bihar, *RRA Notes*, No. 13, August, London.

Scoones, Ian, (1988), 'Learning about Wealth: An Example from Zimbabwe, *RRA Notes*, Number 2, October, IIED, London.

Scoones, Ian, (1992), Wealth Ranking: Insights into Patterns of Rural Differentiation in Southern Zimbabwe, typescript, Sustainable Agriculture Programme, IIED, London.

Sen, Amartya, (1984), *Poverty and Famines, Essays in Entitlement and Deprivation*, Oxford University Press, Oxford.

Sen, Amartya (1988), 'The Concept of Development' in Chenery, H.B. & Srinivasan, T.N. (ed.), *Handbook of Development Economics*, Volume I, North Holland.

Shah, Parmesh, (1990), 'Economic Classification of a Community Using Locally Generated Criteria', *RRA Notes* Number 8, IIED, London.

Shaner, W.W., Philipp, P.F. and Schmehl, W.R., (1982), *Farming Systems Research and Development, Guidelines for Developing Countries*, Westview Press, Boulder, Colorado.

Smith, Shelia and Sender, John, 'Investigating Poverty: An Example from Tanzania', *RRA Notes*, Number 2, October, London.

TISS, (1991 & 1992), *Qualitative Research Methods Newsletter*, Department of Health Services Studies, Tata Institute of Social Sciences, Bombay.

Theis, Joachim & Grady, Heather M., (1991), Participatory Rapid Appraisal for Community Development, A Training Manual Based on Experiences in the Middle East and North Africa, IIED & Save the Children Federation.

Todaro, Michael P., (1989), *Economic Development in the Third World*, Longman, New York.

Vijayraghavan, R., Subramanian, S.R., Pretty, Jules N., and John, K.C. (ed.), (1992), *Participatory Rural Appraisal for Agricultural Research at Aruppukotai, Tamil Nadu*, Department of Agricultural Economics, Centre for Agricultural and Rural Development Studies, Tamil Nadu Agricultural University, Coimbatore and IIED, London.

Warren, Michael D. & Cashman, Kristin, (1989), *Indigenous Knowledge for Sustainable Agriculture and Rural Development*, Gatekeeper Series No. SA 10, Sustainable Agriculture Programme, IIED, London.

INDEX